INCENTIVES VS. CONTROLS IN HEALTH POLICY

INCENTIVES VS. CONTROLS IN HEALTH POLICY

Broadening the Debate

Jack A. Meyer, editor

American Enterprise Institute for Public Policy Research
Washington and London

I thank the Pew Memorial Trust for its support of the seminars and research that made this book possible. I am also indebted to Melinda M. Schwenk for coordinating the organization of this collection of articles into a book.

J.A.M.

Library of Congress Cataloging in Publication Data
Main entry under title:

Incentives vs. controls in health policy.

Based on papers prepared for AEI seminars held in October 1983 and May 1984.
1. Medical care, Cost of—Government policy—
United States—Addresses, essays, lectures. 2. Medical care, Cost of—United States—Addresses, essays, lectures.
3. Medical care—United States—Cost control—Addresses, essays, lectures. I. Meyer, Jack A. II. American
Enterprise Institute for Public Policy Research.
[DNLM: 1. Cost control—methods—congresses. 2. Cost
Control—United States—legislation—congresses.
3. Delivery of Health Care—economics—United States—
congresses. 4. Health Policy—United States—congresses.
5. Reimbursement Mechanisms—congresses. W 74 I36 1983–1984]
RA410.53.I53 1985   338.4′33621′0973   84-29998
ISBN 0-8447-3574-4
ISBN 0-8447-3573-6 (pbk.)

AEI Studies 417

1 3 5 7 9 10 8 6 4 2

Printed in the United States of America

Contents

Foreword

In 1982 AEI's Center for Health Policy Research received a grant from the Pew Memorial Trust to conduct educational seminars for students in allied health fields and to assess new state and local initiatives in health cost management through a companion series of meetings. This volume grows out of papers prepared for the seminars held for doctoral and postdoctoral students in health care policy in October 1983 and May 1984. A volume containing another group of papers from AEI seminars under this grant will be published later this year.

The purpose of this book is to build bridges between issues in health care cost containment and broader public policy issues. The book is designed to place the debate over such questions as market versus regulatory approaches to health care cost management in the broader context of the general advantages and disadvantages of these strategies throughout the economy. The essays suggest that as different as the health sector is from other parts of the U.S. economy, there are important lessons to be learned from the resolution of disputes over prices, costs, and access to service in other sectors.

This book augments the educational impact of the policy discussions convened by AEI. It is designed to inform both today's practitioners and tomorrow's leaders in the health care field and to widen the perspective from which they view the day-to-day controversies over the cost of health care and its quality and availability.

We continue to conduct seminars sponsored by the Pew Memorial Trust, which are intended to be breeding grounds for new concepts and testing grounds for experiments in the health cost field. Students in fields ranging from medicine and nursing to health administration and finance are obtaining firsthand knowledge of how public policy decisions are made. They also have the opportunity to make their own presentations describing research in progress, thereby developing useful skills in communicating new findings and persuading their peers of the policy relevance of their work.

The center's seminars and books have always tried to focus on issues in the forefront of public policy debate. When national health insurance proposals and competing blueprints of federally designed market reforms were the subject of intense debate, the center convened meetings and published books evaluating these proposed alternative strategies. As the focus of interest shifted to more incremental state and local reforms, the center served as a forum for the exchange of new ideas and new models and as a source for the dissemination and transfer of information about new proposals.

This effort also builds on earlier studies at AEI that cut across disciplines and subject matter areas, probing for common themes, common problems, and the common elements of solutions implemented in widely different settings. Two recent AEI volumes, *Meeting Human Needs: Toward a New Public Philosophy*, edited by Jack A. Meyer, and *The Political Economy of Deregulation*, edited by Roger G. Noll and Bruce M. Owen, established our interest in this bridge-building process. This volume continues this interest.

WILLIAM J. BAROODY, JR.
President
American Enterprise Institute

Contributors

RICHARD J. ARNOULD is professor of economics and associate dean, College of Commerce and Business Administration at the University of Illinois, Champaign. He has written extensively on cost containment, regulatory policy, and efficiency in health care and in other sectors of the economy.

PHILIP FANARA, JR., is assistant professor of business and public policy, College of Business and Management, University of Maryland. He has also taught at Indiana University. His current research deals with the effects of price and financial regulation on various industries.

MERTON FINKLER is assistant professor of economics at Lawrence University where he teaches health care public policy, the economics of medical care, urban economics, and public finance. Dr. Finkler has studied a variety of urban planning issues in San Diego, Minneapolis, and Victoria, British Columbia.

CYNTHIA FRANCIS GENSHEIMER was an economist for the Tax Analysis Division of the Congressional Budget Office from 1978 through 1983. She is the author of *Revising the Individual Income Tax* (CBO, 1983) and other articles about the effects of tax reform on families and individuals.

WARREN GREENBERG is associate professor of health services administration at the George Washington University. He has served as visiting associate professor of managerial economics at the University of Maryland and as an economist at the Federal Trade Commission.

CLARK C. HAVIGHURST is professor of law at Duke University and director of the university's Program on Legal Issues in Health Care. He is the author of *Deregulating the Health Care Industry* (1982).

JACK A. MEYER is resident fellow in economics at the American Enterprise Institute and director of the institute's Center for Health Policy

Research. Prior to joining AEI, Dr. Meyer was assistant director of the U.S. Council on Wage and Price Stability. He has written extensively on the financing and delivery of health care.

BRUCE M. OWEN is an economist in private practice in Washington, D.C. Previously he was chief economist of the antitrust division at the Department of Justice and of the White House Office of Telecommunications Policy. He has taught at Duke and Stanford universities and is author or coauthor of many books and articles, including *The Regulation Game* (1978).

CHARLES B. VAN VORST is president of the Carle Foundation Hospital in Urbana, Illinois. He was formerly vice president of operations for the Methodist Hospital in Indianapolis.

JOHN R. VIRTS is corporate staff economist for Eli Lilly and Company, Indianapolis, Indiana. In addition he is a member of the Special Committee on the Nation's Health Care Needs, U.S. Chamber of Commerce. He received his economics doctorate from Indiana University.

GEORGE W. WILSON is associate professor of economics, Central Missouri State University, Warrenton. He is active in health economics research and has published articles in such journals as the *Bell Journal of Economics*, *Business Economics*, and *Health Affairs*.

1
Health Care Policy: Historical Background and Recent Developments
Jack A. Meyer

Since World War II the U.S. government has made a determined effort to improve access to health care. It has bolstered the *demand* for more health services in two ways. First, government programs provide direct health coverage to the nation's elderly, its veterans, and a significant portion of its low-income households. Second, through tax and other policies, the government encourages the purchase by employers of increasingly comprehensive health insurance for their workers.

Increasing Demand and Stimulating Supply

The government established new programs in 1965 to ensure adequate health care protection for the elderly and the poor through the enactment of Medicare and Medicaid. The health care needs of the military and of veterans were also addressed through separate programs.

The government was also active in the 1940s and 1950s in creating a favorable climate for the spread of private health insurance. Employer-provided health insurance and other employee benefits became a mandatory subject of collective bargaining under judicial interpretations of the National Labor Relations Act. Employers' "duty to bargain" interacted with the favorable tax treatment of business outlays for employee health insurance to stimulate the enrichment of group health insurance purchased through the workplace. Under the Internal Revenue Code of 1954, employees were permitted to exclude the full amount of their employers' contributions, without limit, from their own incomes for federal tax purposes.

The postwar period has also been characterized by a stimulative government posture toward the *supply* of health services. The basic

1

thrust of federal policy was to help call forth the resources needed to meet the growing demand for care associated with such factors as rising real incomes, population growth, and the rapid spread of health insurance. The Hospital Survey and Construction Act of 1946 (known as the Hill-Burton Act) was designed to increase the supply of hospital beds and to improve and modernize facilities. Under this act, hospitals had to make care available to all persons in their local area, including a reasonable volume of services for people unable to pay. In addition to stimulating the supply of hospital facilities through Hill-Burton, the government moved to augment the number of doctors through large-scale subsidies for the creation of medical schools and the education of doctors. There has also been a huge increase in the government's support for medical research. The budget of the National Institutes of Health, only about $46 million in 1950, was about $4.3 billion in fiscal year 1984.

Thus, for a considerable portion of the postwar period, the federal government's policy toward health care consisted of a stimulus to demand and a supporting, commensurate effort to increase supply. Not surprisingly, the share of our total resources devoted to health care rose steadily, as the combination of higher real incomes, the spread of insurance, and a consistently favorable government policy led to rapid increases in spending for health care.

Squeezing the System

The essay by John Virts and George Wilson in this volume documents the relatively *small* role played by increases in doctors' fees, hospital charges, and other unit prices in explaining the substantial increases in health care expenditures over long periods of time. Examining a period running as far back as 1929, Virts and Wilson conclude that such factors as growing real incomes, the use of such incomes to purchase a greater quantity and quality of health care, population growth, the stimulus of government programs, and the rise in general inflation throughout the economy explain a very considerable proportion of the growth in overall health spending. Increases in fees and charges greater than general inflation explain a very small amount of the growth, according to Virts and Wilson, and their findings are consistent with earlier studies that disaggregate the growth of health care spending.[1]

Yet, ironically, it was to unit price controls that the federal government turned in the 1970s, as it became nervous about the size of health spending increases that its own policies were feeding. The decade began with price controls on health care, as a part of the overall wage-price controls in force from August 1971 through April 1974. A number of successor formula-based limits on allowable hospital revenue increases under Medicare and Medicaid followed the period of controls. These formulas typically treated all hospitals alike, permitting them the same percentage increase in allowable costs from their base costs. This approach penalizes relatively efficient hospitals and rewards past profligacy.

In addition to capping the natural effects of its own stimulative polices, the federal government actually changed its policy stance a bit in the 1970s with regard to the supply of health care. The chapter by Richard Arnould and Charles Van Vorst notes a turnaround in government policy from stimulating to stymieing the supply of health care. Arnould and Van Vorst describe policies such as certificate-of-need (CON) programs and professional standards review organizations that had the express objective of limiting the supply of facilities and treatments so as to lower spending. Such policies were premised on the twin notions that there were much unneeded capacity and much wasteful medicine and that bodies of local health planners and local peer review boards were well suited to shrink the system without jeopardizing access to health care or its quality. Arnould and Van Vorst also point out the self-defeating nature of underpaying providers of care through suppressing fees and charges under Medicaid. They suggest that if providers react to this underpayment by boycotting indigent patients (a form of limiting the supply of health services), the patients will seek routine care in higher-cost and inappropriate settings, such as emergency rooms.

In my view, shrinking the supply of health care services by having central authorities set allowable charges and guard entry to the health care system will fail to improve consumer welfare. Such authorities cannot know where to strike the balance between cost, quality, and access to care; nor can they possibly accommodate the wide diversity in patients' preferences. Adopting a short-term perspective, centralized authorities will tend to favor quick, discernible results and thus create a bias in favor of cost control at the expense of the future vitality of the health care delivery system. By holding down allowable fees and charges and blocking new entrants into the delivery system, health planners gradually erode the capacity of the system to innovate and modernize. Consumers gain short-term "relief" at the expense of long-term headaches.

The central issue is not whether a system of government price and entry controls *can* succeed in decelerating costs, although success has so far proved elusive. The key question is what the health care delivery system will look like ten or twenty years from now if we

3

squeeze providers through tighter ceilings that do "work," in the sense of achieving a slowdown in spending, without changing the basic inefficiencies and inequities in our health care finance system. I think the system would turn out to be inadequate and inequitable. The real goal is not to freeze health spending at some arbitrary proportion of our GNP but to devise incentives for ferreting out wasteful spending while ensuring the provision of services that an aging population will want and need.

The essay by Clark Havighurst helps to clarify why early forms of government regulation of health care in the 1970s missed the mark. This phase of regulation, according to Havighurst, "served to confirm the dominant view of the health services industry as a unitary system financed by public and private payers committed to reimbursing all . . . costs." Havighurst notes that these early efforts were conservative and ratified the payment ground rules, the monolithic character of the industry, and the locus of decision making that effectively left the consumer out of the picture in health care decision making.

The essay by Bruce Owen places the debate over regulation of health care in a much broader framework. Owen weaves together examples from industries ranging from transportation to communications and finance to illustrate how health care policy debates have their analogues in virtually every other sector of the economy where rate and entry controls have been tried. Our tendency to think of each sector of the economy as unique has led us to presume, mistakenly, that consumer sovereignty, though a laudable general objective, is unrealistic in the particular setting at hand.

Although health care clearly is different, the force of Owen's analysis shows that in a broader sense the issues, the arguments, and the processes of interest group formation are remarkably similar from sector to sector. The importance of this observation is that consumers can learn from our recent experience with regulatory reform in other sectors about the advantages and disadvantages of deregulating health care. A major goal of this book is to illustrate how policy debates in health care relate to broader issues in government regulatory and fiscal policies.

The Buyers Get Tougher

A new phase of government policies toward health care, generally beginning in the late 1970s and early 1980s, goes beyond the mixed-message environment of the 1970s in which government stimulus to the demand for health care was coupled with some second thoughts about a corresponding stimulus to the supply of health care and a spate of rigid spending controls. The new approach is characterized by a relaxation of federal controls on charges and market entry, a movement toward market-oriented incentives for providers to compete for consumers' dollars, and an effort to *reregulate* at the state level an industry that we have begun to *deregulate* at the federal level.

The era of public rate and entry controls is gradually giving way to the use of market power by both public and private sector purchasers of health care. The days when purchasers wrote blank checks for their employees or beneficiaries to fill in for almost any amount and "cash" with any provider are numbered. The federal government, state and local governments, and private employers and unions are all rebelling against the old "allowable cost" approach to establishing payment levels. Health plans featuring prepaid fixed payments or more favorable terms of reimbursement for groups of providers practicing economical medicine are gaining ground. At the same time more orthodox "free-choice-of-provider" and fee-for-service health insurance is undergoing some changes in the direction of greater cost discipline in order to compete. Changes in the organization and delivery of care in response to this new pressure are described and assessed in the chapter by Arnould and Van Vorst.

A more pluralistic landscape is opening up as regulatory barriers to competition gradually recede. But there is a danger that innovative finance and delivery mechanisms will be blocked by the regulation that remains. Merton Finkler's essay warns, for example, of the chilling effect that certificate-of-need programs may have on the establishment of such new delivery mechanisms as free-standing ambulatory surgical centers (FASCs) and suggests some reasons why hospitals might surprisingly favor the "old" regulations such as CON. Although CON may hurt hospitals by blocking some expansion plans, it may also help them more by keeping such would-be competitors as FASCs out of the market entirely. Finkler argues that hospitals may agree to rate setting as a price they have to pay to get CON rules that are tilted in their favor. They may rely on such rules devices to thwart competition that threatens their outpatient departments, which they use to cross-subsidize their inpatient operations.

Owen observes that this process, in which the regulated use the regulations to keep potential countervailing interests from forming, is a central feature of regulation in a variety of industries. The chapter by Warren Greenberg and Philip Fanara suggests that hospitals may use regulation in this fashion. The authors conclude that mandatory prospective reimbursement appears to be more prevalent in states where the market share of nonprofit hospitals is greater. Greenberg and Fanara suggest that nonprofit hospitals might welcome regulation as

5

protection from for-profit hospitals. Allowing only formula-based revenue increases could help freeze the market shares of various types of providers, thereby shoring up the interests of the traditional nonprofit hospitals against the competitive threat from proprietary hospitals.

The hypotheses of Finkler and of Greenberg and Fanara will require further testing to ascertain whether the preliminary evidence, which seems consistent with their predictions, truly reflects behavior. But Owen suggests that the use of regulation to squeeze out developing competitive threats may be quite characteristic of the general regulatory environment. He notes that deregulation poses a threat to those who prefer the "regulation game" to the "competition game" because they have become quite skilled in the former, and he observes that regulatory agencies will not hear from some interests "because regulatory rules destroy the basis on which the interests could be organized."

The Incentives Approach

The essence of the incentives approach is the steering of patients toward cost-effective providers of care. Insurance subscribers and public beneficiaries need to be presented with choices among plans and offered incentives to select a plan that holds down costs while still providing an array of benefits that participants consider adequate.

For such choices to be meaningful, however, consumers require information about insurance arrangements and providers. The supply of useful information and the demand for it are discussed in Warren Greenberg's chapter, which contains some interesting new information on one medical procedure—open-heart surgery—that could be used by patients and doctors in deciding which hospital to use. Greenberg observes a wide dispersion in the distribution of cardiac procedures among hospitals in an area where hospitals differ markedly in the number of procedures conducted. Since hospitals' record of successful outcomes seems to vary positively with the number of cardiac procedures performed, Greenberg concludes that either information about comparative performance is not well known to doctors and patients or factors other than information (such as physician staff privileges) are leading a substantial number of patients to patronize "suboptimal" hospitals.

It is noteworthy that the major buyers of care are beginning to demand that insurers toughen up on reimbursement in the face of strong signals in the opposite direction. Indeed, the presence of the open-ended tax subsidy for the purchase of health insurance reduces the payoff to cost-conscious behavior. This has led some experts to favor a cap on the tax subsidy, which, it is hoped, would increase the value of having employers offer workers a choice of plans with varying price tags. With such a ceiling in place, some employees selecting high-cost plans would have to pay a little extra for them. Critics of this approach suggest that it would not substantially accelerate the movement toward more cost-effective plans and that, if it did so, undesirable side effects, such as an increase in adverse risk selection, would occur.

The tax subsidy issue is analyzed in the chapter by Cynthia Gensheimer. This chapter also places the debate over whether to limit this subsidy in the wider context of the debate on whether to broaden our tax *base* in order to hold down tax *rates*. Employee benefits such as health insurance are only one of many tax subsidies that could be limited as an alternative to federal tax surcharges, postponing tax indexing, or excise and payroll tax increases.

The New Regulation

An alternative to the use of market forces to contain health care cost increases is the use of "new regulation" to put pressure on providers. Foremost among the new regulatory programs are state all-payer systems, in which states prescribe hospital rates paid by third-party payers, including both private payers and Medicare and Medicaid. Clark Havighurst argues in his chapter that although the all-payer proposals emphasize equity among payers and prevent Medicare, Medicaid, and Blue Cross from using market power to avoid their "fair share" of costs, the real purpose is to "ensure each hospital a fixed level of payment and enough resources that it can continue at least some of its customary education, research, and indigent care."

Havighurst interprets these programs as an effort to preserve hospitals' ability to cross-subsidize these activities and apportion the hidden "tax" more equitably among hospitals. But he contends that the all-payer mechanism cannot permanently meet this goal because regulation cannot permanently ensure a flow of patients to hospitals charging inflated rates to support unremunerative services. He suggests that "all-payer regulation cannot fairly distribute or permanently sustain the burden of such services as long as patients and insurers remain free to take their business to institutions that do not impose the same hidden tax." Havighurst suggests that we consider a promising alternative to the all-payer approach—allowing competitive forces to erode inefficient cross-subsidies and substituting explicit, direct subsidies for activities such as research and uncompensated indigent care, activities that would otherwise be underproduced.

7

This point deserves greater emphasis. The development of an adequate, fair "safety net" is a vital accompaniment to a desirable movement away from a regulated health care market. Deregulation and direct subsidies for low-income and high-risk individuals go hand in hand. This means that rate setting and a solution to the problem of funding indigent care do *not* have to accompany each other. In my view, it is regulatory overkill for states to establish the rates at which all payers reimburse hospitals in the name of dealing with the indigent care problem. An all-payers approach, like its long line of regulatory antecedents, freezes current inefficiencies in the hospital sector, propping up high-cost providers and handicapping more efficient ones.

Both new incentives and new regulations are now cropping up around the country, as the buyers rebel against the old cost-pass-through mentality. National "plans," of either a regulatory or a market variety, are languishing, and it seems clear that, for now at least, the federal government is not going to solve the health care cost problem. The creative tension and competition between market and regulatory approaches at the local level is probably healthy, and under either approach doctors, hospitals, and other providers are "feeling the heat."

In summary, government policy toward health care has gone through several phases and has now entered a period of substantial flux and varied experimentation. New models of cost containment that bear little similarity to the rate and entry controls formerly used are being tried and tested in both the public and the private sectors. Fiscal constraints have led public payers to clamp down on reimbursement, and private sector purchasers are following suit. The government is limiting the stimulus to both the demand for health services and their supply. As the private sector also tightens up, there are demands for new rules of the game, but these are being tested locally rather than through national controls.

Notes

1. See, for example, Mark S. Freeland and Carol Ellen Schendler, "National Health Expenditures: Short-Term Outlook and Long-Term Projections," *Health Care Financing Review* (Winter 1981), p. 103.

2

The Debate over Health Care Cost-Containment Regulation: The Issues and the Interests

Clark C. Havighurst

The earliest attempts by government to control health care costs sought to prevent "unnecessary" capital investments and the provision of "unnecessary" services. As these efforts disappointed expectations, more comprehensive forms of regulation were proposed and were adopted in several states. Although enthusiasm for such regulation fell off for a time as "procompetition" proposals were given a hearing, regulation of hospital rates by the states is once again being strongly urged. The themes of the current debate over regulation differ somewhat from those heard in the proregulation push of the late 1970s. This chapter, after providing some background, reviews the reasons for this new impetus, the arguments being advanced, and the interests at stake. As in all debates over regulation, industry groups with an economic interest in the outcome are the dominant voices, and their arguments are frequently selective and misleading, revealing the true issues only if listened to with a discerning ear.[1]

Deficiencies of Early Cost-Containment Efforts

Early cost-containment initiatives designed to curb unneeded capital investments and inappropriate use of services were unlikely to succeed because they were based on a misconception of the cost problem and an overestimate of government's political ability to contest health care spending decisions taken in the private sector. These strategies were acceptable politically only because they addressed symptoms of the problem rather than its fundamental causes and did not seriously threaten the customary autonomy of established interests. Indeed, early cost-containment measures served to confirm the dominant view of the health services industry as a unitary system financed by public and private payers committed to reimbursing all but demonstrably unreasonable costs incurred either by providers in providing or by patients in purchasing covered services. Because they did not seek to alter the monolithic character of the industry or to change payment ground rules, the early government controls were essentially conservative, constituting only a small shift in the locus of decision-making authority in the system.

Several specific misconceptions of the cost problem were reflected in these early measures. Certificate-of-need (CON) laws regulating providers' capital investments, for example, neglected the likelihood that, as long as open-ended revenue sources were available to be exploited, costs incurred by providers and patients would, like a partially constrained balloon, simply grow in unregulated directions. Experience under these regulatory programs suggests that any savings in capital and related costs were indeed offset by increases in labor costs and in capital spending that regulation did not reach.[2] Moreover, both CON laws and programs to discourage unnecessary care through peer review were based on the assumption that the cost problem is one of spending on facilities and services that are essentially worthless, both to society and to the patients being treated. Unfortunately, although some useless spending does occur, the real problem lies in spending on services that, though beneficial, are not sufficiently so—given the small probability or slight value of the health benefits sought or the existence of offsetting risks—to justify the outlay.[3]

Both CON laws and programs to control unnecessary use also proceeded on the unexamined assumptions that publicly designated experts could determine how and how much of society's resources should be spent on health care services and could make their official judgments stick.[4] Unfortunately, policy makers underestimated the ability of providers to rationalize high spending, either by ignoring the trade-off between benefits and costs altogether or by exaggerating the likelihood or value of the health benefits to be obtained. Faced with professional justifications for particular spending, politically accountable health planners and regulators found it difficult to deprive patients of allegedly obtainable benefits or to veto any desirable capital project that did not clearly duplicate existing facilities. In a political world where a professed commitment to unstinting provision of health services is a useful symbol of humanitarianism, it is difficult for publicly accountable decision makers to challenge authoritative professional judgments and to insist on close calculation of benefit-cost ratios. Health planners, regulators, and peer reviewers have seldom found it easy to say no to more and better health services in circumstances where nearly everyone else was inclined, largely because of the presence of open-ended insurance, to say yes.[5]

The Movement toward Hospital Rate Setting in the 1970s

As the ineffectiveness of early forms of government cost containment became increasingly obvious throughout the 1970s, policy makers began to consider more far-reaching regulatory proposals. Several states adopted hospital rate-setting regulation, and in 1977 the Carter administration proposed a far-reaching bill that would have imposed a fixed percentage limit on the annual growth of hospital costs; roughly, the revenues of each hospital would have been allowed to increase each year at no more than the overall rate of hospital-cost inflation plus 1 percent. Although the bill left a major loophole for the automatic pass-through of higher labor costs, its other features suggested a new potential for effective cost containment.

In particular, the proposal's formula-based approach stood in striking contrast to previous cost-containment efforts, which had relied on explicit public determination of the appropriateness of capital and treatment costs incurred. Because the proposed constraint was purposely arbitrary and concerned only with a hospital's bottom line, it promised not to entangle the government in balancing specific health benefits against dollar costs and thus to increase the regulators' political capacity to be rigorous. By shifting the responsibility for rationing specific services to the newly constrained providers of care, the proposal had the potential virtue (at least from the standpoint of cost containment) of allowing the government to escape the political burden of confronting providers over specific outlays.

Ironically, the same arbitrariness that promised to make the Carter proposal somewhat effective in containing costs proved to be its undoing. For two years interest groups scrambled to get Congress to correct various actual or alleged inequities in the bill, thereby eliminating much of its potential bite. Congress finally defeated what was left of the proposal in 1979. This action put an end, at least for the time being, to federal efforts to solve cost problems by regulation. The advent of the conservative Reagan administration ensured that no further regulatory proposals would be forthcoming from the executive branch for some time to come.

The Context of the New Debate over Regulation

Since the defeat of the Carter bill, the debate has shifted to new ground. The federal government is no longer primarily interested in controlling costs industrywide and has concentrated on controlling the costs of its own programs, Medicare and Medicaid. As a major payer for services, the federal government has begun to phase out the strategy of directly challenging costs incurred by providers and is moving toward a payment system based not on retrospectively determined costs but on price. Under the Social Security Amendments of 1983, the Medicare program introduced a prospective schedule of payments for hospital services based on diagnosis. In contrast to the old cost-reimbursement approach, prospectively fixed payments will impose on hospitals the burden of controlling their own costs so that they can live within, or maximize their profit from, the fixed DRG (for diagnosis-related group) allowance.

Other payers, both public and private, are following the government's lead toward more aggressive buying and are beginning to negotiate with individual hospitals and physicians over the price of specific services. Medi-Cal, the California Medicaid program, has required hospitals to bid competitively for the right to serve its beneficiaries. Many private purchasers, especially large employers, that had previously assumed either that health care costs were beyond their control or that the government would sooner or later take the needed regulatory actions are now uncertain of government help and are beginning to challenge providers on their own. As both governments and private payers begin to act for the first time as prudent buyers rather than as passive intermediaries, providers are responding in competitive ways, particularly by organizing or joining preferred provider organizations, whose members agree to provide services for less or to submit to special cost controls.

In the current climate, proposals for direct governmental regulation of hospitals spring from concerns quite different from those of the Carter years. The regulatory programs of the 1970s proceeded from the nearly universal assumption that market forces were not capable of keeping costs within an appropriate range. Providers were seen as autonomous and immune from price competition. Insurance coverage was thought of as an absolute barrier preventing cost-containment pressures from ever arising on the demand side of the market or being communicated to providers. In addition, the government's role as payer for over 40 percent of U.S. health care was perceived as making costs its inevitable regulatory responsibility. Today, however, the government and other major payers are finding ways to address their own cost problems by steering patients to providers whose efficiency and prices make them better buys. Whereas regulation was previously favored by those who feared (or at least alleged) that market forces would not work, it is now attracting interest among those who fear that such forces may work altogether too well.

Cost Controls Only for Public Programs or Industrywide?

Because of cost trends in the Medicare and Medicaid programs, the federal government has consistently been a leading exponent of some form of health care cost containment. Before the Carter administration, Washington policy makers were largely content to foster controls on capital spending and on utilization and to tinker with Medicare cost-reimbursement formulas. The Carter proposals for hospital cost containment, however, were designed to address other aspects of the problem and to control costs for private payers as well as for the federal government. An important issue has been whether the federal government should assume responsibility for its own costs alone or should adopt an industrywide regulatory strategy to control costs for other payers as well.

An important tenet of the Carter proposal was that controls should not adversely affect the quality and quantity of care received by federal beneficiaries unless those controls similarly affected privately financed care. Although the Carter administration rationalized industrywide regulation in part on the ground that private payers needed federal help in confronting providers and forcing them to be efficient, there was at least some sentiment for denying the middle class the right to enjoy its desired standard of care unless it was willing to finance the same standard for beneficiaries of federal programs. Careful appraisal of the plan suggests that equity for federal beneficiaries was the dominant goal in tying public and private regulation together.

The current Republican administration has been significantly less concerned about equity and more concerned about the costs incurred by the federal government. Its policy has been to address costs without regard to a possible widening of the gap between the care received by the general public and that received by federal beneficiaries. Adoption of the administration's DRG payment system for Medicare did not, however, present the equity issue sharply. Enacted as an amendment to the bill implementing the widely heralded compromise saving the social security system from imminent bankruptcy, the prospective payment system—the most fundamental change in the Medicare program since its enactment—moved through Congress with little opposition. Though passed at a time when concerns about federal deficits tended to outweigh concerns about equity, the final bill required that the shift to the new payment system be budget neutral

13

and therefore did not, on its face, allow the government to realize an immediate saving at the expense of beneficiaries.

The shift to a payment schedule did, however, threaten to reduce the average quality of care by forcing cutbacks by high-cost hospitals— arguably the ones offering superior quality—while permitting lower-cost hospitals to receive more than they had previously been allowed for possibly inferior services. In the long run, of course, the government hopes that removal of the cost-escalating incentives inherent in retrospective cost reimbursement will slow growth of expenditures and allow Medicare beneficiaries to be adequately served for less money.

While the Reagan administration was adopting a new way of paying for Medicare services, it was also moving to allow the states greater flexibility in structuring and administering their Medicaid programs. Recognizing the budget pressures on state governments, the administration counted on the states to take aggressive cost-containment action and thus save the federal government substantial matching funds that it is committed to pay. Recent federal policy toward the Medicaid program is thus another reflection of the prudent purchaser strategy. Focusing almost exclusively on budget considerations, however, it has reflected little concern that the care received by public beneficiaries may be not only unequal but in many cases inadequate.

Although it is sometimes argued that the Reagan administration, concentrating on public program outlays, lacks a coherent policy toward private health care costs, it is possible to discern a policy that, though consisting primarily of "benign neglect," is in some ways constructive. For the administration, private health care costs are a private problem, to be solved not by regulation but by competitively inspired innovation in organizing delivery systems and in designing and administering health insurance coverage—all with the object of reintegrating, either contractually or organizationally, the financing and delivery of services. The greatly stepped-up pace of change in the private sector since the defeat of the Carter cost-containment bill indicates, at the very least, that a federal policy of denying regulatory responsibility for private costs is not an irresponsible abdication.

The Reagan administration's proposal to put a ceiling on currently unlimited federal tax subsidies for employer-purchased private health insurance is an affirmative policy designed to inspire employers to purchase more cost-effective coverage. In theory, capping this subsidy would cause people to buy insurance packages or other kinds of protection that feature an optimal balance between essential pooling of risks and the higher consumption and costs that such financial protection inevitably induces. In the absence of an unlimited subsidy, the prevailing level of insurance—and the resulting level of private spending—would be much harder to characterize as excessive. The purchase of broad coverage would no longer be inspired by the desire to pay as many routine health expenses as possible with dollars that had not been subjected to heavy income and payroll taxes. Even if some privately purchased coverage still seemed poorly designed, its high costs would be borne largely by those who had freely chosen to purchase it.

For these reasons, the administration's policy toward private sector health care has some theoretical validity. Even without enactment of the tax change, it is already paying dividends in the form of innovation and intensified price competition. When coupled with the recent movement to apply the antitrust laws to the health care industry, the market-reform, incentive-oriented approach to containing private health care costs is a promising strategy.

The Problem of Cost Shifting

The most common criticism of recent federal health policy is that single-minded pursuit of budgetary savings in the operation of public programs has imposed undue and unfair burdens on certain elements of the private sector, exacerbating their cost problems. Specifically, it is alleged that the stricter Medicare reimbursement policies of recent years, the new DRG payment system, and state Medicaid cutbacks have resulted in payments to hospitals that are inadequate to cover the actual cost of the care provided. Any such underpayments would have to be made up by hospitals through a combination of reduced quality or intensity of care, increased charges to other payers, and diversion of discretionary resources from other uses. Although the extent of government underpayments is debatable because of the vagaries and imprecision of cost accounting, there is general agreement that many hospitals are indeed facing serious deficits under the new payment policies of federal and state governments.

The current financial problems of hospitals are in large measure a consequence of their historical practice of relying on liberal payments from all third-party payers, including governments, to support services that the market cannot support. As long as payers were unable or unwilling to resist paying more than the marginal cost—that is, a competitive price—for covered services, nonprofit hospitals were able to cross-subsidize such generally desirable activities as manpower training, research, and the care of patients who could not afford to pay for the care they received and did not qualify for support under any public program. As the government has become less free with its reimbursements, many hospitals, particularly nonprofit ones, are not

15

willing, or do not consider themselves free, to discontinue these activities. Therefore, wherever possible, they have sought to finance continuation of these good works by charging even higher prices to those patients who, usually because they have indemnity insurance, can afford to pay and do not question their bills.

The term "cost shifting" has been coined to characterize the federal government's alleged policy of paying less than the full cost of caring for its beneficiaries. The government is said to have shifted some of its costs to the hospitals, which in turn—to whatever extent they have been able to get away with it—have shifted their unrecovered costs to private payers. Although this may be an accurate description of what has occurred, the central issue is not whether the government is in fact getting services for its beneficiaries at prices below average or marginal costs. The more important fact is that the government's new aggressiveness as a buyer is threatening to upset the delicate system of cross-subsidies that has developed over the years to meet important needs. Moreover, the government is not the sole culprit in creating these troubles, for many private purchasers are also having good success in obtaining hospital discounts in competitive markets. Indeed, however liberal or illiberal government payment policies may be, it seems only a matter of time before increasing competitive and cost pressures on private insurers and health care providers will eliminate most of the system's historical capacity for cross-subsidization.

Although "cost shifting" may not be the right name for it, a problem certainly exists. Increasing aggressiveness on the demand side of increasingly competitive markets for both health insurance protection and insured services is indeed having disruptive effects on the supply side of those markets. Private insurers that have heretofore borne the cost of the hospitals' internal subsidies without much complaint now find themselves being exploited more than ever before. Many hospitals are running out of such payers of last resort, however, and, as a consequence, many former beneficiaries of internal subsidies, particularly the poor, are feeling real hardships.

Deregulation and the Destruction of Cross-Subsidies

The troubles being experienced in the health care industry are essentially indistinguishable from dislocations that occur in industries newly subjected to deregulation. Although the health care industry has never been subject to comprehensive regulation by a single agency similar to the Civil Aeronautics Board or the Interstate Commerce Commission, it has long been a regulated industry in the sense

16

that its members have been systematically protected against the operation of normal economic forces. The de facto exemption from the antitrust laws that the industry enjoyed until the late 1970s permitted many private arrangements that effectively foreclosed price competition.[6] Over a long period, the medical profession, claiming special expertise and high ethical principles, succeeded in establishing its cultural authority and its political influence and in preempting decision-making authority over a wide variety of economically important matters.[7] In addition, organized providers, by directly controlling or otherwise influencing the nature and behavior of health insurers, were able to insulate themselves from cost pressures that would normally be transmitted from the demand side of the market.[8] Providers succeeded in establishing in law, in the operation of public and private financing plans, and in the public mind their preferred view of the health care sector as a monolithic self-regulating system, not a competitive industry.

A common feature of most industries subject to comprehensive economic regulation is cross-subsidization of some services out of monopoly returns earned by the regulated firms on other business. To ensure that regulated firms can generate the excess revenues needed for such internal subsidies, regulation must protect them against competition by maintaining entry controls and prohibitions against price cutting. The quid pro quo for these protections is the regulated firms' willingness to plow at least some of their profits back into serving other customers at prices below the cost of service. Some, though certainly not all, of the services supported by such cross-subsidies would be deemed vital by society and would be discontinued or not adequately provided if the subsidy were removed.

The cross-subsidies that regulation fosters are financed by what is in effect a hidden tax paid by one group of consumers and earmarked for the benefit of others. This method of redistributing income and financing public services has been called taxation by regulation, and it is in such widespread use that it is hard to argue that it is anything but a legitimate exercise of governmental power.[9] Nevertheless, it is worth observing that the incidence of the "tax" may be quite inequitable and that the redistribution of income is not necessarily always in the direction of the less well off. Moreover, the usual constitutional steps for levying a tax are bypassed, and neither the need for the particular subsidy nor its amount is established through the normal process of legislative authorization and appropriation. Public officials may also have little occasion to monitor expenditures or the performance of the subsidized tasks. Although worse forms of financing public services can be imagined, taxation by regulation cannot be regarded as an

17

optimal means of defining and meeting public objectives.[10]

Cross-subsidies in the health care industry are a clear instance of taxation by regulation. Indeed, they may constitute the most entrenched, most extravagant, and least closely supervised government-tolerated use of private monopoly to generate resources for public purposes anywhere in the U.S. economy. By the same token, the destruction of this system of internal subsidies by increased cost-consciousness and competition may threaten dislocations and hardships more serious than any that have been associated with deregulation in other industries. The issues that must be addressed in deciding whether to let market forces continue to take hold in the hospital industry are thus very similar to those that have arisen in other deregulation debates and must be taken at least as seriously.

To be precise, of course, the specific policy question is not whether to deregulate the health care industry but whether to "reregulate" it. Just as beneficiaries of internal subsidies in other regulated industries have routinely made common cause with the providers of subsidized services in opposing deregulation, a coalition of health care interests now supports explicit regulation of hospitals as a way of replacing old bulwarks against competition that are rapidly crumbling.

Reregulation—All-Payer Proposals

The regulatory agenda that now has the most support contemplates state prescription of hospital rates payable by third-party payers, both public and private. Most all-payer proposals anticipate that no financing plan will be able to negotiate favorable rates with a particular institution. Some proposals, however, leave room for health maintenance organizations (HMOs) and other organized health plans to bargain for discounts. Although the federal government is, of course, free to refuse to pay the state-prescribed amount, federal law allows the Medicare program to grant waivers to states with rate-setting programs that undertake to regulate effectively enough that Medicare can expect to incur costs no higher than it would incur under its own payment rules.

Although the emphasis in all-payer proposals is on equity among payers and on preventing Medicare, Medicaid, and Blue Cross plans from using their buying power to avoid their fair share of the cost burden, the real focus is on the hospitals themselves. Rate setting may be done in various ways,[11] but is likely to ensure each hospital a fixed level of payment and enough resources to continue at least some of its customary education, research, and indigent care. The all-payer proposals should be understood as an effort, first, to preserve hospitals' ability to cross-subsidize desirable activities and, second, to apportion the "tax" needed to support these activities more equitably among the hospitals' paying customers. Consumers paying health insurance premiums to any payer of all-payer rates and taxpayers supporting any public financing program paying these rates will all be contributing something to support the hospitals' continued ability to provide services for which no one else is willing to pay.

Although it is hard to dispute the desirability of equity in the apportionment of the costs of the hospitals' internally subsidized projects, regulation of this sort cannot permanently ensure such equity. The burden of education, research, and indigent care is not borne at all equally by hospitals, and payers will contribute to a hospital only to the extent that those whom they insure use it. Those hospitals with the greatest need for funds (and thus the highest markups) will find paying patients gravitating elsewhere under the influence of copayments and other insurer-developed incentives. This flight will accelerate in a vicious circle if an institution seeks to load its unrecovered costs on fewer and fewer non-cost-conscious patients. In short, regulation cannot permanently guarantee that a hospital will retain enough paying patients at inflated rates to support a heavy commitment to providing unremunerative services. All-payer regulation cannot fairly distribute or permanently sustain the burden of such services as long as patients and insurers remain free to take their business to institutions that do not impose the same hidden tax.

Although all-payer regulation coupled with strict CON regulation could certainly slow the breakdown of the existing system of cross-subsidies, it would interrupt the progress now being made toward establishing competition as a force for appropriate spending in the health care sector. Before regulation is accepted, we must fully evaluate the alternative policy, now beginning to take hold, of letting competition enforce efficiency throughout the system. Though necessitating new explicit subsidies to support hitherto cross-subsidized vital services that the market will not support, a policy of continuing on the present deregulatory course has much to recommend it.

The Issues and the Interests

The new debate over state-administered hospital rate setting has immense implications for the health care industry. A brief summary of the positions of the participants in the deregulation-reregulation debate is presented here as a way of focusing on the issues and the interests at stake. As is typical in debates over deregulation, most of

19

the parties are engaged in special pleading, and their arguments must be sifted before they can be taken seriously as policy recommendations.

The Federal Government. The Reagan administration's positions on state rate-setting regulation are conflicting in some respects. Although the administration favors a competitive market for health services, it is also committed to states' rights and is thus apt to be deferential to state decisions to regulate, even if those decisions undercut the federal policy of promoting competition. Nevertheless, the administration has not been eager to grant waivers of Medicare payment rules to states with hospital rate-setting programs. A new Democratic administration would probably be more supportive of state initiatives. Ironically, the presence of all-payer regulation in a number of states seems likely to weaken the long-term political prospects for federal hospital regulation along the lines of the Carter proposal. It appears, for example, that the existence of federally approved all-payer systems in such important states as Massachusetts and New York prevented active opposition to the administration's DRG payment system by important Democratic legislators from those states.

The greatest failing in current federal policy appears to be the neglect of the problems that underinsured persons will confront as competition destroys the industry's capacity to cross-subsidize their care. The Reagan administration's tax cuts and war on federal spending on domestic programs have left the federal government without a realistic capacity to provide new public funds to replace the hidden subsidies of the past. The claim that the states bear the responsibility for meeting these needs is hard to accept in view of the new financial burdens that state governments bear as a direct consequence of other federal policies. The lack of federal and state money to meet these needs certainly adds some weight to the case for moving, even at some cost, to preserve the health care system's ability to finance itself. One promising alternative to a regulatory policy would be to use the revenues from the proposed cap on the tax subsidy for private health insurance to offset the side effects of competition.

The States. The states have frequently been attracted by rate-setting proposals as a way of restraining the growth of Medicaid costs. Their new ability under federal law to pursue prudent purchaser strategies in administering their Medicaid programs, however, may give them a new and even more promising cost-saving alternative. Nevertheless, equity considerations may point toward regulation. Moreover, a state perceiving severe and increasing burdens on county and other public hospitals for indigent care may see rate setting as a way of meeting at least some of these institutions' revenue needs, thereby shoring up the system's capacity for cross-subsidization and relieving public budgets. A CON law that could be used to prevent patients from forsaking hard-pressed institutions for new facilities might make regulation a feasible way to delay the need for new state or local funds.

Commercial Health Insurers. The leading advocate of all-payer regulation is the Health Insurance Association of America, representing commercial health insurers. These traditional insurers are poorly situated to resist the cost shift because they have little ability to negotiate prices with hospitals. Attributing their lack of bargaining power to the small percentage of patients that any one of them insures in any given market, they have for some years sought an antitrust exemption that would allow them to confront local hospitals collectively. It is far from clear, however, that their problems arise solely from low market shares; certainly there are some markets in which a single insurer of one or more large employment groups would possess ample bargaining power if it knew how to use it. Instead, the insurers' ineffectiveness lies in their inability (or unwillingness) to influence their insureds' choice of hospital, an inability that allows hospitals to ignore the insurers' pleas for lower prices. In short, the product that most commercial insurers are selling is poorly designed, and it is likely to fare poorly in the increasingly competitive climate that is beginning to develop. Capping the tax subsidy for private insurance would simply accelerate the switch to more efficient coverage.

Because commercial insurers are in a poor position to resist the cost shift by hospitals, they have embraced all-payer regulation as a way of sparing themselves the usual competitive consequences of selling an inefficient product. Many of them are beginning to develop innovative plans that create useful incentives for cost containment, but most of them would prefer to be spared the risks of competing in a rapidly changing environment. Although they have the ability to fight back through innovation, they appear anxious to avoid joining the battle.

Blue Cross. In many markets Blue Cross plans enjoy substantial discounts in paying for hospital services. They are naturally not anxious to lose this competitive advantage through the establishment of all-payer regulation. Whether a Blue Cross plan that enjoys favorable rates does so simply because of its efficiency and effective use of its buying power is not entirely clear, however. Some such discounts are collectively bargained with state hospital associations and, not being

21

the result of competition, may be subject to challenge under the anti-trust laws. Nevertheless, Blue Cross plans have increasingly disen-gaged themselves from the hospitals that collectively sponsored their creation and are for the most part favorably positioned to compete in the new environment. Their opposition to all-payer regulation is un-derstandable.

HMOs and Other Competitive Health Care Plans. Locally organized health plans competing with traditional insurance programs would be handicapped if bound to pay state-prescribed all-payer rates. Rather than oppose such regulation, however, HMOs and similar plans are likely to lobby for exceptional treatment that allows them the option of buying hospital services for their subscribers on preferential terms. (Federal law permits a Medicare waiver even though a state offers such plans special treatment.) The ability of such plans to control their subscribers' hospital choices stands in sharp contrast to the practice of traditional insurers.

Hospitals. The attitude of a hospital toward all-payer rate setting de-pends on its circumstances. The leading trade associations, however, generally oppose such regulation. The Federation of American Hospi-tals, representing investor-owned institutions, is particularly opposed to regulation of any kind, reflecting its members' faith in their ability to compete effectively and their lesser involvement, as proprietary institutions, in providing cross-subsidized services of the sort that raise the costs of their nonprofit competitors. For-profit institutions appear to have the management ability to prosper under a variety of market circumstances. The existence of this vigorous and politically effective subgroup of hospitals, eager for more competitive elbow-room, has been important in making deregulation politically feasible.

The American Hospital Association (AHA), representing a broad spectrum of hospitals, also opposes rate regulation and supports the administration's proposed tax cap. These positions apparently reflect a belief by a majority of AHA members that, even with changed incentives, hospital competition will generally not be cutthroat and that the plight of particular hospitals can be addressed by other means. Hospitals must perceive that the federal precondition for granting a Medicare waiver—that it not result in higher costs to Medi-care than would be incurred under the usual reimbursement rules—practically guarantees that any state all-payer system will be extremely stringent for hospitals.

Public hospitals and nonprofit community hospitals having de facto responsibility for a large indigent population are naturally attracted by regulation. Although teaching hospitals frequently provide a large volume of uncompensated services, they do not necessarily support regulation. To the extent that they provide tertiary or higher-quality care not available from other nearby institutions, they can count on a continuing flow of patients and some freedom to earn monopoly returns with which to subsidize their unremunerative efforts in teaching, research, and indigent care. How a particular institution sizes up its long-term competitive position and the likely attitude of regulators toward its special needs will determine its position on regulatory proposals.

Employers and Unions. Major purchasers of health insurance are not unanimous in their positions on state regulation of hospital rates. Employers that have some control over the design of their employees' group insurance coverage will probably prefer do-it-yourself cost containment. Other employers, however, unable to persuade unions to accept increased cost sharing or limitations on freedom of choice, are likely to look to the state.

Some employers and most union leaders appear to use their health benefits plans as a symbol of their identification with their workers' welfare. Where this attitude toward health insurance prevails, any retreat from liberal coverage is virtually unthinkable. As a consequence, employers and union leaders, concerned about high costs, are led to support state regulation as a way of taking away from the workers some of the liberal benefits they have so freely granted. This kind of behavior on the part of those charged with representing the consumer's interests suggests how the current tax subsidy for employer-purchased insurance spares employers and unions from the need to reeducate workers about health insurance and to buy coverage that induces efficient behavior by both patients and providers. Because employers and unions have agendas of their own in dealing with the issues here, their support for regulation is probably a poor indication of where the public interest lies.

Consumers. The consumer interest likely to be best represented in the political debate over state hospital regulation is that of the beneficiaries of cross-subsidies. Though preferring explicit public financing, these groups and their political allies may perceive that they can do better in the short run by relying on the hidden taxes that regulation can generate than by counting on new government financing.

The interests of other consumers and taxpayers are, as usual, not likely to be heard in proportion to their aggregate importance. Unions and employers that claim to speak for consumers may have interests of their own. Consumers themselves, long accustomed to believe that their interest lies in having the broadest possible entitlement to insured services, are unlikely to be enlightened by the political debate. It is hard to believe that consumers' welfare, particularly their interest in efficiency, is likely to be served, except fortuitously, as decisions on regulation are made through the rough-and-tumble of interest group politics.

Conclusion

The regulation of hospitals is being advocated for a variety of reasons, but the ultimate issues are essentially two. First is the problem of choosing a vehicle for making the myriad difficult benefit-cost trade-offs that must somehow be addressed in providing for health care needs out of society's limited resources. On the one hand, regulation contemplates, if not explicit central decisions on how resources are to be used, at least centrally imposed resource constraints that force providers to ration services. On the other hand, the procompetitive strategy now being given a limited trial contemplates that consumers and their agents, in deciding how much of their resources to dedicate to health care, will impose constraints and cause spending patterns to be shaped according to their preferences.

The second overriding issue is, of course, the choice of a vehicle, either implicit taxation by regulation or explicit taxes and income redistribution, for meeting the health care needs of less fortunate citizens. These basic policy choices obviously depend on difficult empirical and value judgments relating to overriding concerns about equity and efficiency. Attempts to choose between or reconcile these often competing values are, of course, never easy.

Whether regulation or deregulation is the better health policy is an issue that can be and probably will be endlessly debated. Unfortunately, however, continuing the nation's flirtation with cost-containment regulation without final resolution, one way or the other, is not without substantial costs. If, on the one hand, this choice could be resolved so that the likelihood of government regulation was insubstantial, many purchasers of health services would move aggressively to protect themselves against higher costs, and many providers would move to achieve efficiencies and develop organizational arrangements that would position them for success in an increasingly cost-conscious environment. On the other hand, a continuing political prospect that regulation will be introduced encourages the belief that the government is in charge (even if it has not yet acted), discourages private decision makers from investing in innovations that government action might make obsolete tomorrow, and diverts energies and resources away from cost containment and into anticipating and attempting to shape the regulatory environment. The contrast in the rate of progress in private cost containment before and after the 1979 defeat of the Carter cost-containment proposal strongly suggests that regulation can have a powerful inhibiting effect on change even if it is not enacted. For this reason we must hope, even against the political odds, that a final choice of a basic health policy can soon be made.

Notes

1. See Roger G. Noll and Bruce M. Owen, *The Political Economy of Deregulation: Interest Groups in the Regulatory Process* (Washington, D.C.: American Enterprise Institute, 1983).

2. See Clark C. Havighurst, *Deregulating the Health Care Industry* (Cambridge, Mass.: Ballinger, 1982), chap. 3; and Paul L. Joskow, *Controlling Hospital Costs* (Cambridge, Mass.: MIT Press, 1981).

3. See Clark C. Havighurst and James F. Blumstein, "Coping with Quality/ Cost Trade-offs in Medical Care: The Case of PSROs," *Northwestern University Law Review*, vol. 70 (1975), p. 6; and William B. Schwartz and Paul L. Joskow, "Medical Efficacy versus Economic Efficiency: A Conflict in Values," *New England Journal of Medicine*, vol. 299 (1978), p. 1462.

4. Many supporters of such laws were more interested in legitimizing high costs than in containing them. See Sallyanne Payton and Rhoda M. Powsner, "Regulation through the Looking Glass: Hospitals, Blue Cross, and Certificate-of-Need," *Michigan Law Review*, vol. 79 (1980), p. 203.

5. See Havighurst, *Deregulating the Health Care Industry,* chap. 2.

6. See Clark C. Havighurst, "The Contributions of Antitrust Law to a Procompetitive Health Policy," in Jack A. Meyer, ed., *Market Reforms in Health Care* (Washington, D.C.: American Enterprise Institute, 1983), p. 275.

7. See Paul Starr, *The Social Transformation of American Medicine* (New York: Basic Books, 1983); and Clark C. Havighurst, "Decentralizing Decision Making: Private Contract versus Professional Norms," in Meyer, *Market Reforms in Health Care*, p. 22.

8. See Clark C. Havighurst, "Professional Restraints on Innovation in Health Care Financing," *Duke Law Journal* (1978), p. 303; and Lawrence E. Goldberg and Warren Greenberg, "The Effect of Physician-Controlled Health Insurance: U.S. v. Oregon State Medical Society," *Journal of Health Politics, Policy and Law*, vol. 2 (1977), p. 48.

9. Richard A. Posner, "Taxation by Regulation," *Bell Journal of Economics and Management Science*, vol. 2 (1971), p. 22.

10. See Jack A. Meyer, *Passing the Health Care Buck: Who Pays the Hidden Cost?* (Washington, D.C.: American Enterprise Institute, 1983).

11. See Joskow, *Controlling Hospital Costs.*

3

Interest Groups and the Political Economy of Regulation

Bruce M. Owen

This chapter examines the role, motives, and behavior of organized interest groups in regulatory proceedings. It weaves together illustrations from a variety of industries but focuses especially on the regulation of the health care industry. Comparisons and analogies between health care regulation and government policies affecting such industries as transportation, communications, and finance are scattered through the chapter to show how issues arising in one sector of the economy correspond to disputes in other sectors.

It may strike some readers as cynical to observe that interest groups have an important influence on policy making. As we shall see, however, the regulatory process was consciously designed not only to recognize the activities of interest groups but also to make positive use of the information they provide. The major conclusion of the chapter is that policy makers must recognize the special incentives of participants in the process. The information provided by interest groups can then often enlighten public policy. Policy makers must also recognize that some points of view are not likely to be represented effectively in the process.

I begin with a brief survey of the role of interest groups as based in political theory.

The Role of Interest Groups in a Federal System

The American form of government is based on rationalist, egalitarian principles. One is the primacy of individual rights over the rights of

This paper is adapted from chapter 2 of Roger G. Noll and Bruce M. Owen, *The Political Economy of Deregulation: Interest Groups in the Regulatory Process* (Washington, D.C.: American Enterprise Institute, 1983). My original coauthor, Roger Noll, deserves much of the credit for what is interesting herein and no blame for this adaptation.

the state. Another is the principle of consent—that government powers should be derived from general agreement among the citizenry that those powers are legitimate.

The Constitution, reflecting these principles, contains several provisions that strongly affect the procedures followed by government officials in making decisions. It affirms, for example, a right of citizens to participate in government decision making, limits the power of government to confiscate wealth, and establishes the foundation for challenging government decisions in the courts.

The Founding Fathers, in setting up a democratic government structured to allow extensive participation by citizens in policy making, were aware of an important pitfall in this form of government: the possibility that government power could be captured by special interests. The constitutional problem as seen by the founders was to set up a process in which citizens' participation was guaranteed but in a manner that protected against powerful special interests.

In number 10 of the *Federalist Papers*, James Madison analyzed "factions," or interest groups, and their potentially harmful influence in a nonfederal system of government:

> By a faction I understand a number of citizens, whether amounting to a majority or a minority of the whole, who are united and actuated by some common impulse of passion, or of interest, adverse to the rights of other citizens, or to the permanent and aggregate interests of the community.[1]

Madison and his colleagues sought to design a system of government that would be able not merely to resist the harmful effects of factions but to harness their energy to the common good:

> The regulation of those various and interfering interests forms the principal task of modern legislation and involves the spirit of party and faction in the necessary and ordinary operations of government.[2]

The idea was simple: create a federal representative government in which each faction or interest was represented but had relatively little power. That government, properly designed, could balance the various special interests while providing adequate opportunities for each to persuade a majority of the merits of its position. No one faction could succeed in tyrannizing the rest.

A similar set of concerns underlies the design of the regulatory policy process. Policy is made in the context of organized persuasion by competing interest groups with something to gain or lose from the outcome. These interest groups are often composed of industries, industry segments, individual firms, and labor organizations. Consumers and the general public are not as well represented. Even consumer groups or public interest groups often have interests that, though allied with consumers' interests, may differ in important ways. The positions of environmental groups, for example, may not reflect consumers' interest in obtaining goods and services at reasonable costs even when they do reflect consumers' interest in a clean, healthy environment.

Interest groups provide regulators with information, analysis, and argument that, properly used, can serve the interests of the general citizenry. Much of the information and analysis would be difficult or impossible for policy makers or their staffs to compile independently. Interest groups hire able advocates and analysts whose work would otherwise have to be done by the same staffs that help the decision makers evaluate the arguments. When competing interest groups are forced to provide the decision makers with costly data, analysis, and argument, the policy decision is likely to be a better one, provided that the decision makers recognize and take account of the biases that arise from the special advantage or disadvantage that each group expects from the proposed action.

Each group naturally takes positions and makes arguments that it regards as economically beneficial to itself. The regulator's job is to sift these arguments, to identify those that both arise from self-interest and are concerned wholly with self-interest, and to discover valid arguments that arise from self-interest but are concerned also with the interest of consumers. Regulators must also recognize that some legitimate interests may not be represented in the debate—perhaps because regulation has prevented their formation.

The constitutional principles of broad representation, rights of participation, protection of private property, and due process have all had major effects on the way the regulatory agencies make decisions. The agencies are usually very specialized, dealing with a sharply focused set of policy issues that are rarely of widespread political salience. Moreover, agencies affect the distribution of wealth in society not by direct expenditures of funds but by creating the ground rules by which the economy operates. The agencies are thus an unimportant part of the budgetary process, easily overlooked in the range of government activities even if their impact is great. For these reasons they easily become obscure and subject to excessive influence by special interests.

One form of protection against this outcome is the formal procedure by which agencies reach decisions. The constitutional principles discussed above have been interpreted by the courts and codified as procedural rules for agency decisions. These include quasi-judicial rules regarding evidence and participation in the process and the requirement that agency decisions be based on information and analysis acquired through a relatively open process. Agencies must show that their decisions respond reasonably to a statutory mandate, recognize the evidence presented, and have a substantial basis in the record of the proceeding that led to them. Moreover, people dissatisfied with an agency's decision have the right to appeal it to the federal court system for failure to adhere to these standards.

These rules have two somewhat opposing effects. First, because the process is formal and legalistic, it is expensive for participants. Its costliness militates against broad representation. Second, it protects against an orientation toward special interests by the agencies because it requires them to pay attention to all who are represented. One key to the performance of this process, then, is whether the first effect is sufficiently weak that broad participation nonetheless emerges.

The Forms of Economic Interests

The economic interest of a group in a debate over regulatory policy can take several forms. The most straightforward example, and the most widely analyzed and recognized, is an industry that uses regulation to establish a form of cartel that is to some extent insulated from attack on antitrust grounds. State licensure of health professionals by boards composed of such professionals is one example of such a regulatory scheme. The effect is to raise entry barriers and prices. Because true cartels are relatively easy to detect and politically vulnerable, regulation rarely produces such a result for very long. A more modest, more attainable objective for a group is to seek some special advantages that it could not obtain if it were faced with the discipline of normal market processes.

Among producer groups, common examples are rules that establish cost-based minimum prices to buttress profits during periods of slack business, government assistance in averting competitive risk (for example, loan guarantees), and entry barriers that protect existing firms. All regulatory agencies have had experience with this phenomenon. Certificate-of-need (CON) regulation of medical facilities is designed precisely to create entry barriers to new competition or to output expansion by existing competitors. Whether or not CON regulation is beneficial to consumers in the long run, its primary or immediate beneficiaries are the economic interests associated with existing health care facilities.

The regulations of the Federal Communications Commission restricting the importation of distant television signals by cable systems are another example. The rules included a total freeze on cable television during an extended period in the late 1960s and early 1970s and created important actual or perceived benefits to local broadcast stations by limiting competition from cable television services.[3] The cable rules were originally motivated by a desire to protect viewers' interest in local programming, just as CON regulation was designed to hold down health care costs. But groups of local stations that benefited had an interest in opposing deregulation and advocated that the restrictions be retained. The commission eventually found that the cable television regulations were not beneficial to consumers.

Suppliers of goods and services to an industry normally have a stake in its regulation. They can be expected to oppose a cartel in the regulated industry because cartels restrict output and thereby reduce the industry's demand for inputs. But some suppliers, such as industrywide unions, may take the opposite view if they have monopoly power over the industry. Then the gains derived from regulation by the cartel can be extracted in turn by the monopolistic supplier.

Suppliers may also have reason to favor regulation in a competitive industry that succeeds in setting prices above the competitive level but does not control other forms of competition. Regulated firms can then be expected to compete by improving product quality, which may require even greater use of some inputs than price competition.

Examples of suppliers taking positions for these reasons abound in the transportation sector. The Teamsters union strongly advocates trucking regulation, and railroad workers' unions tend to favor regulation of the railroads. These unions have been especially adept at capturing a share of the excess profits derived from the anticompetitive effects of regulation, either through very effective wage bargaining or through featherbedding. Airline pilots opposed deregulation of airlines on the specious ground that competition would erode safety. But research has demonstrated that regulation created competition in the frequency of flights—causing airlines, for example, to schedule more flights with fewer passengers per flight. Pilots feared that deregulation would reduce demand for pilots as higher load factors enabled the same number of passengers to fly on fewer flights. The effect of deregulation on safety, if anything, is to increase it.

Opportunities arise for groups of users as well as suppliers to seek advantage through the regulatory process. In regulated industries supply shortages are normally dealt with by administrative rules setting priorities among users rather than by letting prices increase until the market clears. Groups of users seek to attain higher priority for themselves than that enjoyed by others. During the oil supply shortages of 1973 and 1979, for example, agricultural interests were especially effective in receiving allocations of fuel at essentially no reduction from previous free market levels.

Regulation also creates opportunities for groups of users to seek special breaks in the price structure of regulated firms. In nearly all regulated industries, firms provide a variety of products or services, some of them to a particular, identifiable industry or other organized group. Such a group has an interest in making sure that the prices it is charged are as low as possible. Because regulated prices tend to be based on costs, the debate is often over costing principles. Regulators are forced to undertake a process that sellers would otherwise undertake for themselves in response to the market, namely, to allocate among various products or services the common costs of the business. Each user group can be expected to advocate a costing principle that allows the service it uses to be priced favorably.

An example of the common cost problem arises in the health field. Overhead and other common costs of medical facilities can be allocated more or less arbitrarily among services, patients, and third-party payers. As Medicare regulations, for example, increasingly exclude provisions for such costs as research or bad debts, the burden of meeting them falls on private insurers, who naturally oppose further increases in their costs.[4] Thus commercial insurers have supported all-payer controls on both government and private sector reimbursement rates to achieve "equity" through regulation.

Both suppliers and users have stakes in decisions by regulators about the nature of the regulated product. While regulated firms provide a variety of services, the economics of production normally preclude the possibility of tailoring services to suit exactly the most desired characteristics of every user. Regulation provides a forum in which the characteristics of the service can be debated, whether it be the number of hours of community service or locally produced broadcasting or the number of ounces of meat in an airline meal. These regulations determine which customers will be best served by the particular configuration of attributes in a regulated product and which suppliers will be most helped by these constraints.

Users and suppliers alike, as well as regulated businesses, have a stake in how regulatory rules allocate business risks. Businesses must make long-term capital investments based on only partly predictable economic variables such as customers' tastes, the state of the economy, the possibility of product and process innovation, and the prices of inputs and competing products. Regulatory rules decide not only how suppliers, users, and regulated firms will fare if things work out as expected, but also how they will bear the risks and rewards of

31

unanticipated events.

In an unregulated world, two common means of coping with risk are risk-pooling contracts and vertical integration. Both give a buyer and a seller a means to guarantee stability in a business relationship, either by agreeing to the terms of a continuing flow of transactions long in advance or by merging the activities of buying and selling.

In a regulated environment, whether a firm can use these strategies and, if so, in what form are justifiably matters for regulators to decide: without regulatory scrutiny regulated firms can sometimes use long-term contracts and vertical integration to preclude regulators from attaining their policy objectives. Such arrangements can lock in a particular pattern of business decisions and prices that regulators might wish to change in the future. They can also help a regulated firm escape a constraint on the overall rate of return of one part of the business.

An additional feature of risk-spreading arrangements, however, is that companies that are not party to them generally must assume greater risk. This is a part of the argument of commercial health insurers, who are shouldering a disproportionate share of uncompensated care (such as bad debts and charity care), relative to Medicare and Blue Cross. Both of these actors, however, claim that they enroll many people who would otherwise become "bad debt" patients.

These risk-spreading arrangements do not remove the risk from an industry; instead businesses agree to share with their suppliers or customers the brunt of an unexpected event. Obviously, these other groups would like to prevent this from happening and, if possible, to obtain regulatory rulings that transfer the burden of risk to still others. In the case of health insurance, commercial insurers seek state hospital rate-setting mechanisms to keep the burden of risk from being shifted to them.

Regulation as an Element of Corporate Planning

The regulatory process is fully capable of conferring rewards and benefits on persuasive and effective interest groups. Firms must recognize this in their planning and in their development of business strategies. Indeed, a firm that discovers a way to benefit from regulation can come to have a tremendous economic stake in perpetuating a regulatory mechanism. Firms orienting their planning to take advantage of regulation will have a different mixture of revenue sources, investment projects, and so on from that of firms that do not take strategic account of regulation. Deregulation would leave such firms in a potentially embarrassing competitive position.

The airline industry provides examples of firms that had learned to prosper under the route-awarding and fare-setting process of the Civil Aeronautics Board. Such firms had a particularly difficult time coping with the competitive pressures of a deregulated market. Similarly, many trucking concerns used the anticompetitive certification process of the Interstate Commerce Commission (ICC)—which placed the burden of proof on a new entrant to show the economic necessity of certification—as part of their strategic plans. The ICC mechanism tended to protect the certified routes from competitive attack and thus led to a different pattern of route development than would have occurred in a free market.

Deregulation poses a threat to another kind of firm or group: one that simply prefers the regulation game to the competition game because it happens to be better at the former. A firm that has special attributes valuable in regulated environments—skill in advocacy or political connections, for example—will tend to capture a larger market share and higher profits under regulation than under a fully competitive market. Such firms will constitute a particularly effective interest group opposing deregulation, even though the group would not exist but for regulation. Other firms may simply be familiar and comfortable with life in a regulated world. Pan American, for example, was the "chosen instrument," or U.S. flag carrier, in international commercial aviation, having a status much like the nationalized carriers of other countries. It was subjected to very limited competition from other American carriers and among the international companies operated under the protective umbrella of the International Air Transport Association (IATA), the cartel of international airlines. Such firms—and even their customers—may regard a movement away from the quiet, predictable life of regulation as unduly or unnecessarily risky, even if tangible benefits can be expected from deregulation.

Even regulation that is neutral in its effects on consumers and on the competitive vigor of an industry is likely to produce a different distribution of economic benefits among firms than would exist in a free market. Firms that are doing well under regulation have something to lose—their market position—and are much more likely to constitute a well-financed and organized group opposing deregulation than firms at the bottom of the heap. In the debates about airline deregulation, for example, the major passenger carriers commanded the most attention, and most, such as American, Eastern, Delta, and TWA, opposed deregulation. United, the largest domestic carrier, initially opposed it but switched positions when it perceived itself to be in a stronger growth position than other carriers and unlikely to be awarded new routes under regulation. Many small, vigorous airlines that came to flourish under deregulation, such as New York Air, Midway, and People Express, had less of a voice in the debates, although two of them, PSA and Southwest, were major participants because they had succeeded in the two largest deregulated intrastate markets, California and Texas.

Regulation as a Creator and Destroyer of Interests

The policy analysis of any proposal to repeal a rule or to deregulate must obviously take into account the self-interest of those presenting information and arguments. It may not be so obvious to consider the possibility that some interest groups may actually have been created—and others destroyed—by enactment of the rule being debated. Some interest groups may not be participating in the debate because regulation has caused them to disappear; others may be participating that have an interest or even an existence that is artificial because it was created by the very regulations in question.

Not all the interest groups that participate in a regulatory debate would exist in the absence of the rules whose repeal is proposed. Moreover, agencies will not hear from some interests because regulatory rules destroy the basis on which the interests could be organized or because the groups are officially neutral and therefore silent. In the health area, for example, the so-called freedom of choice and antidiscrimination laws in many states block insurers from offering special rates to patients using the more efficient preferred provider organizations (PPOs). Because of these laws, no such organizations have been in existence to participate in the policy debate. A similar story could be told concerning the various possible "hybrid" health delivery organizations that lie between health maintenance organizations (HMOs) and traditional systems. Where such hybrid services do not exist, their voices are obviously absent from health policy debates.

Regulations that have any effect at all—good or bad—necessarily cause the structure of the economy to depart from its unregulated state. Some firms have more business; others have less. Some firms and products do not exist that otherwise would; others exist that would not in a free market environment. Regulation has such effects regardless of whether its net effect is beneficial to consumers. Indeed, regulation sometimes transfers wealth from one group of consumers to another, just as it can redistribute profits from one group of firms to another. When these effects can be anticipated, they motivate participation in the debate over regulatory policy by the potential gainers and losers.

34

Often the effects are either intended by policy makers or reluctantly accepted as a necessary cost of achieving a desired objective. But effects can also be unanticipated and inadvertent. Some groups may receive unintended benefits and thereby have a vested interest in perpetuating the regulation. Indeed, it may be an inadvertent regulatory benefit that defines an interest group.

The effect of this phenomenon is that a regulation can be more strongly advocated once it is in effect than it ever was when it was being considered. The initial source of participation will be the anticipated effects on the groups organized to participate in the debate. When regulation is in effect, the losers will have been weakened, and some will have disappeared. Meanwhile, interests created by unanticipated side effects will advocate continuation of the regulation, although they did not initially participate. Consequently, the effort required by an agency to overturn an outdated or mistaken regulation can be far greater than the effort required to establish it in the first place, because outside interests are motivated to provide more evidence and analysis in support of a regulation conferring actual benefits than in support of a proposal conferring only anticipated benefits. This phenomenon increases the responsibility of the regulator to ensure that a balanced range of views is heard in the evaluation of a proposal to deregulate.

An example of these phenomena can be seen in the economic history of health care reimbursement systems in the United States. Organized medical interest groups exemplified by the American Medical Association (AMA) behaved essentially as cartels for many years, with political influence so powerful as to command government-sponsored entry barriers and bans on innovation. The Blue Cross and Blue Shield plans were set up very largely by and on behalf of the medical establishment. Doctors collected the money to pay doctors, and there was little opportunity for innovative services or competition. When the federal government finally instituted the Medicare and Medicaid programs, they simply mirrored Blue Cross and Blue Shield: doctors remained sovereign. The unique institutional relationship between service provider and bill payer that characterized the Blue Cross plans was largely copied in the government programs, reflecting the political power and influence of the traditional medical interest groups. These same groups were for many years successful in barring reimbursement and even licensing of novel and more efficient health delivery systems such as HMOs. Indeed, HMOs were eventually sanctioned only by direct government intervention, and hybrid systems are still opposed.

Consider, as another example, the self-regulation—sanctioned by the Securities and Exchange Commission—of the New York Stock Exchange, which before 1975 allowed the members of the exchange to fix brokers' commissions.[5] This regulation prevented price competition and set a uniformly high price for stock brokerage service. It also encouraged competition in services and image-oriented advertising.

Large institutional traders, whose business was especially profitable to brokers at the fixed prices, constituted a special interest group with an incentive to oppose regulation initially and to advocate deregulation because they and their customers (for example, pensioners) would tend to benefit the most from market-clearing prices. Stockbrokers initially favored regulation and opposed deregulation: regulation made them better off by enabling them to act as a cartel to enrich themselves at the immediate expense of high-volume purchasers, such as mutual and pension funds. By keeping prices above the competitive level, regulation not only made some brokerage firms especially profitable but also allowed some inefficient and badly managed firms to succeed. Before regulation no interest group of inefficient firms existed. But regulation created such an interest, one that subsequently fought hard against deregulation.

Banks offer another illustration of how an interest group has been created by regulation. The Federal Reserve Board's Regulation Q keeps interest rates paid to small savers on passbook accounts artificially low. Meanwhile, to the extent that interest-rate regulation reduces the interest paid on savings below competitive levels, banks can lend out the funds at interest rates above the regulated level, pocketing the difference between the two rates. Thus an advantaged group of financial institutions is created with an interest in opposing deregulation. The losers are small savers and unsophisticated consumers.

Like banks, savings and loan institutions have been required by regulation to pay below-market rates of interest on passbook accounts. But unlike banks, savings and loan institutions are required to place most of their assets into mortgage loans. Some believe that competition among savings and loans for a limited market may force them to pass on part of their lower costs from passbook accounts in lower mortgage rates benefiting the housing industry, although there is little evidence that they do so. In any event, there was a time when savings and loans were the only source of long-term home mortgage financing. For this reason, whether rational or not, the construction and housing industries have come to believe that they have a stake in preserving regulatory restrictions on the savings and loans. The depression-era policy makers who initiated the regulations surely did not fully anticipate the new suburban bedroom communities and housing-related employment that would be created. Yet such regulations inadvertently created gainers who are now part of the resistance to deregulation.

Consider, as another example, the bias in petroleum regulation in favor of small refiners. During the period of extensive regulation of prices and allocations of crude oil and petroleum products, small refiners were given greater access to relatively cheap domestic crude oil and were subjected to less restrictive controls on refinery products. This bias encouraged the survival and entry of inefficient small refineries that would otherwise have been unable to compete with large refineries. It created a powerful interest group that derived important benefits from perpetuating petroleum regulation, without regard to the effect on the nation's energy supply.

The airline industry before deregulation offers still another example of an interest group created by regulation. Carriers with profitable routes to which entry by competitors was barred by regulation had an incentive to oppose deregulation. So did smaller communities that came to believe—for the most part incorrectly—that regulation caused airlines to serve them.

Airline regulation undoubtedly produced a different route structure than deregulation, because factors other than economic efficiency were used to decide which firms could serve which routes. In principle, deregulation could have caused the immediate abandonment of many routes. This would have taken place if regulation had created some extremely profitable routes by severely controlling not only the number of airlines allowed to serve them but also the number of flights that each could offer and by allowing the favored few to charge monopoly prices. Deregulation would then have caused the excluded lines to flock to these routes by switching planes from other, less profitable ones. In fact, regulators never required airlines to continue to serve routes that lost money; even if planes had initially been reallocated away from small towns, other carriers or commuters would have instituted service. The fears of small communities that they would lose all air service were thus not well founded.

The existence of formal route awards may have created the illusion that regulation made service possible. Or small communities may have perceived, correctly, that they had little to gain from deregulation. Since the airlines serving them did not appear to be making excessive profits or giving them excessive service, any small chance of losing service was not worth the risk. The overall effect of deregulation, however, was clearly beneficial; it led to greater efficiency, lower fares, and better service for most passengers.

Resistance to Changed Circumstances

Most regulatory agencies were established during the depression of the 1930s or even earlier. The conditions and perceptions that led to much of that regulation are no longer relevant, just as there is no longer an energy crisis giving rise to a rationale for the fifty-five-mile-per-hour speed limit. Technology has changed in some industries. Clean air goals are perhaps not best served by the old automobile emission standards. The structure of other regulated industries is no longer the same. In the television industry, for example, actions to permit the growth of cable and pay television, to allow direct satellite broadcasting, and to allocate the UHF band to television have gradually eroded the market power of networks, thereby weakening the case for restraining them. Similarly, a better-informed population is perhaps less in need today of the professional licensing restrictions imposed on health practitioners. Experience since the 1930s has taught us that, whatever the theoretical merits, serious inefficiencies are often the practical result of regulation. In some cases, such as trucking, direct comparison with unregulated markets has even allowed us to measure the social costs of regulation. Yet proponents of regulation often ignore or discount these changes.

One of the costs of regulation is that it creates a process that can be used to resist economic change. Regulation must be invoked to approve changes in the nature of regulated services or the way in which they are offered and consequently retards the response by a regulated industry to changes in its economic and technical environment. The presence of regulation thus confers benefits on those who have an incentive to resist economic change. Indeed, one type of interest group created by regulation is composed of firms and industries that have become obsolete or that benefit from obsolete services. Their primary strategy against deregulation is to obscure the fact that the market judgment about them has turned negative.

An example of this can be found in some of the opposition to railroad deregulation. The initial impetus for regulation came from some railroads, which wanted to restrict competition on routes between major cities, and from some rural interests and small communities, which wanted to put an end to monopoly pricing for short-haul traffic. As the costs and demand for rail service changed, however, two kinds of service became unprofitable at any price: passenger service (principally serving the same big cities that in an earlier era had benefited from competition and opposed railroad regulation) and routes predominantly serving manufacturing shippers on small community sidings. Railroads, facing severe financial problems, sought to abandon these services.

In an unregulated industry, changes in the economic environment cause changes in prices and services. Customers respond to new and more convenient or more economical opportunities by altering their consumption patterns. But in the world of ICC railroad regulation, abandonment of services required regulatory approval. The communities or customer groups that received unprofitable service had an interest in continued regulation. Moreover, regulation had given them rights they would not enjoy as buyers in an ordinary market: the right to continue to receive subsidized services and to require someone else to pay, in part, for services they consumed. They retained this right until a formal regulatory decision ending the privilege could be made and upheld. By creating a right to be served unless defeated in a political-legal contest, regulation created an interest group favoring preservation of its historical status in the face of changing economic circumstances that questioned the very wisdom of regulation.

Railroads are not alone. Microwave and satellite technology transformed the economics of intercity telecommunications, making competition feasible where it was not before. The telephone industry fought hard to preserve the regulated monopoly that was created when other technology was dominant. As a result, entry and competition for intercity services were retarded.[6] It was twenty years or more before the opposition of the entrenched industry could be overcome. Indeed, the newly independent Bell operating companies are still fighting to limit intrastate toll telephone competition.

Regulation of the programming and commercial practices of radio stations was based on the notion that private interests should not determine what the public hears from a few sources. Since the FCC was created, however, the number of radio stations has grown from a few hundred to nearly 9,000. Competition for listeners is extensive, serving to limit excessive commercialization and providing diversified programming responsive to listeners' demands. By the 1970s the FCC's radio regulation was thus no longer needed because competition had become more effective than regulation. Yet proponents of regulation, mainly political and activist groups whose interests were served by forcing radio stations to air their messages, ignored the structural changes in the market and the degree to which the regulations were anachronistic and ineffective.

Strategic Use of Regulation

A desire to use the regulatory process to handicap one's competitors is common. One dramatic example is the apparent attempt by large ocean freight customers to use shippers' conferences as a device to put their smaller competitors at a disadvantage. Incumbent firms can use the regulatory process to gain an advantage over actual and potential competitors. In a number of regulated industries, competitors that desire to enter the industry, expand their geographic scope, or lower their prices can be opposed in regulatory proceedings. Regulated firms can use the regulatory mechanism to impose costs and delays on their would-be competitors, thereby deterring entry and restricting competitive responses to noncompetitive conditions.

In television markets, another good example, the networks are but one of several distribution channels. Programs are also distributed to stations as first-run or off-network properties, and first-run syndicators that use satellite distribution look increasingly like networks. For creative products such as motion pictures, distribution channels include pay television, networks, theaters, and cassettes or discs as well as over-the-air broadcasts. Management and coordination of the distribution of creative properties are functions in which television networks, Hollywood distributors, and others compete with one another. One effect of the FCC's rules on financial interest and syndication is that the networks are largely restrained from participating in this process. This reduction in the number of competitors, if it benefits anyone, benefits the remaining firms—the Hollywood studios and major syndicators who fought successfully to retain the rules in 1983.

A number of industries exclude or delay competitors by effectively using entry barriers. The telecommunications industry has witnessed lengthy proceedings to determine whether competition would be permitted. The telephone industry, especially AT&T, vigorously opposed competition. In the airline and trucking industries incumbent firms have also participated actively in the regulatory process to limit competition. Existing firms have opposed entry proposals and have usually favored rules that make it more difficult for new firms to obtain approval from regulators. Similarly, price reductions have been effectively challenged in both industries by competing firms, thereby raising the costs and reducing the profitability of attempts to engage in price competition.

Using the standard-setting process to competitive advantage is another regulatory strategy available to firms in some regulated industries. Setting environmental standards is one example. In 1977, for instance, Congress passed legislation establishing standards to control emissions of sulfur oxides from new electricity-generating plants. After much debate, the rule finally established by the Environmental Protection Agency (EPA) required stack-gas scrubbers that would remove a given fraction of sulfur oxides from stack gases. That is, the same percentage reduction in sulfur emissions had to be achieved no matter what the initial sulfur content of the coal was.

Coal can, however, differ dramatically in sulfur content, western coal having especially low amounts of sulfur. For many regions, therefore, the most cost-effective approach to clean air is to burn low-sulfur coal from the West and spend relatively little on cleaning the stack gas.

Obviously, this fact did not please eastern coal interests, which lobbied successfully for standards that called for a straight percentage reduction of even the smallest amounts of sulfur. All new plants would need the same scrubbing equipment. These standards reduced the incentive for utilities to pay the higher transportation costs to acquire western coal. An unfortunate side effect was to worsen air quality, because scrubbed gases from the burning of eastern coal are dirtier. The high-performance scrubbers required by the EPA are very expensive. Regulation has created an added incentive to keep in service older, dirtier, and less efficient plants that are exempt from the standards. And scrubbers in practice frequently fail, further worsening air quality.

A better approach would have been to set an absolute standard for air quality, giving the power plants some latitude about how to achieve it. But because eastern coal mining is fully developed and located in relatively populous states while western coal is a largely undeveloped resource located in states with very low populations, the eastern coal interests had the political influence to get the standard they wanted.

Attempts have been made to use safety standards for similar anticompetitive purposes. The American bicycle industry proposed safety standards for bicycles before the Consumer Product Safety Commission (CPSC).[7] The proposed standards imposed design features that would effectively have excluded foreign bicycle manufacturers. Unaware of these features, the CPSC adopted the standards but rescinded them after an uproar from bicyclists made it aware of the problem.

Consider, again, the securities industry's attempt to retain regulation that prevents banks from competing to underwrite municipal bonds. This is a striking case of an industry group seeking by regulation to prevent a potentially more efficient group of competitors from entering the market.

There is an analogy in health care delivery: the medical establishment's insistence on what Havighurst calls a "uniform standard of care."[8] This leads doctors, for example, to oppose licensing and hospital privileges for nurse-practitioners and other innovatively trained or

41

qualified health professionals.[9] Limitations of this sort are the result of pressure from medical interest groups. In neither the securities case nor the network program case do the parties seem to be seeking to divide excess profits among themselves. The fight is over the stability of markets and market shares. Something similar is involved in the insistence on a uniform standard of health care.

Factors Affecting Successful Representation

Effective advocacy, whether in the political process, in the courts, or before a regulatory commission, costs money, often a substantial amount. Indeed, the very procedures that implement constitutional principles guarding against factionalism can make it expensive to be heard, and some points of view may not be adequately expressed. Some general statements can be made about the kinds of groups that are likely to be well represented.

Self-Interest. The first observation to be made about participation in the regulatory process is that a participant must have an important reason to become involved. Almost always the interest is personal: the decision is perceived to have an important effect on the participant's welfare. Usually the interest is even narrower: the welfare at stake is the participant's economic position, and the interest of the participant is in receiving a favorable decision about prices, service quality, or rights in the regulated market. Truly disinterested participation to advocate a general public good, though not unheard of, is extremely rare. The number of significant political and legal processes is large, and effective participation requires money and time. Consequently, most people will elect to participate only in processes in which their direct, personal stake is high. The American Medical Association, for example, will lobby to protect its interests, but prospective patients will not. The dilemma of the regulator, not unlike the dilemma of the political representative or the jurist, is to identify the public interest amid a chorus of self-seeking arguments.

Group Size. Even among self-interested groups, not all will be equally well organized and represented. A second important factor explaining participation in the regulatory process is that, other things equal, groups with few members are better able to organize and express their views than groups with many members. A group that successfully obtains a regulation or rule beneficial to its members cannot usually limit the benefits flowing from the regulation to members who have contributed financially to the advocacy effort. This gives members of the group an incentive not to contribute: each can expect to get a free ride by obtaining the benefits of successful advocacy without having to bear any of the costs.[10] In large groups the incentive is especially strong because no single member will perceive that it has an important influence on the total effectiveness of the group. But to the extent that a significant fraction of a group's members tries to be free riders, the ability of the group to finance its advocacy efforts adequately will be severely hampered.

Groups with few members are usually better able to overcome the free rider problem. The smaller the number of members, the greater is each member's share in the benefits realized by the group. Because of this greater stake in successful advocacy, individual members of small groups are more likely to perceive that the chance of group success depends on their own individual efforts. Moreover, smaller groups can more easily monitor the contributions of each member. Groups with relatively few members are thus in a better position to apply peer pressure to members who do not contribute their fair share to the effort. This characteristic tends to make oligopolies and monopolies more effectively organized than competitive industries and the latter better organized than their customers.

The principle is illustrated by the extensive lobbying and political activities of the steel industry in pursuing restrictive trade policies. Because it has historically been an oligopoly, the steel industry has not faced a serious free rider problem. A dozen or so firms capture nearly all of any benefits the industry receives from protectionist legislation. Steel customers, because they are less concentrated, are harder to organize, although one group, automobile manufacturers, could surely be an effective force for free trade in steel if it did not have its own problem of coping with foreign competition.

The free rider problem is not insuperable. It merely implies that, other things equal, it is an advantage to have fewer members in an interest group. Of course, other things are not always equal, and interest groups with many members are sometimes very successful in advancing their members' interests, and the AMA is again a good example.

The analysis thus far has assumed that individual members of the interest group voluntarily contribute to an advocacy effort. Some interest groups with many members are successful because they are able to compel contributions from their members or because the group has already been effectively organized for another purpose. The Teamsters union and the maritime unions, for example, have been prominent opponents of deregulating the trucking and ocean shipping industries, respectively. Both unions have many members, but union dues are not voluntary contributions; so the unions do not face a free rider problem in obtaining funds for advocacy. Another example is the American Automobile Association. Many of its members join because of the services it offers: roadside repairs, free maps, and the like. Yet the organization actively lobbies to advance what it perceives to be the interests of motorists.

The relation between the size of an interest group and its chances of succeeding in obtaining regulation favorable to its members is also affected by the size and strength of the opposition. The relative, not the absolute, abilities of competing groups to organize their efforts are important in determining the effect of interest groups. This is perhaps best illustrated by the success of competitive industries composed of many firms in retaining beneficial laws, rules, and regulations. The successful lobbying efforts of the trade associations of such industries are explained partly by the fact that their opponents are often taxpayers and consumers, who are much more numerous and face even greater free rider problems than the producers. Truckers' support for the fifty-five-mile-per-hour limit to increase the demand for trucking services is a good example. Farming and ocean shipping are also examples of structurally competitive industries that have successfully retained not only federal subsidies but anticompetitive legislation and regulation that benefit industry members at the expense of less well represented taxpayers and consumers.

The success of agricultural interests in obtaining favorable legislation and regulation illustrates another way in which the effects of the free rider problem have been overcome. The system of political representation devised by the Founding Fathers to protect against factionalism actually promotes it in one way because it discriminates in favor of sparsely populated states. South Dakota has the same number of senators as New York. As a result, interests that are concentrated in sparsely populated states are significantly overrepresented politically. Because there is a negative correlation between the population of a state and the relative importance of its agricultural economy, it is not surprising that farm interests are clearly heard, especially in the Senate. The substantial attention that federal regulators devote to prices and service in sparsely populated areas is probably at least in part a response to the same political reality.

Size of the Stakes. Another factor that can attenuate the effectiveness of groups with many potential beneficiaries is the absolute size of each member's interest in the outcome. If each member stands to gain only a small benefit, the chances are that a successful lobbying effort cannot be organized. If, however, the absolute stakes are very large for each member, advocacy is more easily funded, even in the face of large numbers. The lobbying efforts of the maritime industry can be explained partly by the fact that the continuation of government subsidies is probably crucial to the very survival of many firms in the domestic industry.

The ability of a group to become organized for effective political participation depends on the degree of homogeneity of interest among the group members. Groups in which the primary objective of each member is essentially the same and can be simply stated and in which each member has a similar stake in the outcome will be easier to organize and more effective. Homogeneous groups need not spend a great deal of time ironing out differences and finding a mutually acceptable statement of purpose and need not fear defection of members who do not get what they want.

In the political sphere, this characteristic is exhibited by single-issue groups that effectively oppose gun control, abortion, and the teaching of evolutionary theory, even though all three of these activities are supported by a majority of the population; this characteristic is exhibited as well by the lack of success in forming an effective group for tax reform, an issue of almost universal interest but too complex and too heterogeneous to be an effective focus of political organization.

In the regulatory sphere, this phenomenon tends to favor producer groups at the expense of consumer groups. Labor organizations and trade associations largely agree that restrictions on competition among themselves enhance their economic interest. Consumers, in contrast, have widely varying stakes in decisions about price and service quality in any particular industry. If organized at all, buyers are usually fragmented into groups with relatively homogeneous interests and may orient their participation as much toward gaining advantage over other customer groups as over the regulated producer group.

Some organizations, such as "public interest" law firms or consumer organizations, regard themselves as representing the interests of all or most consumers in regulatory processes. But often they do so imperfectly at best because of two major problems. First, these groups must worry about their own survival. The regulatory process gives them a source of power they would not otherwise possess to affect market performance and, to the extent that regulators consider their views, to obtain leverage over other groups. Public interest groups can be an instrument for intervening in government processes in behalf of otherwise unrepresented groups; hence they can be expected to be biased in favor of regulatory solutions and against market solutions,

45

because their influence will be greater under a regulatory regime. Consumers who believe in such solutions will find themselves well represented by public interest groups; consumers who believe, however, that they would be better served by less regulation are not likely to be as well represented.

A second problem confronting public interest groups concerns their relation with their constituency or client groups. Consumerism is primarily a middle-class movement. Even among consumer activists, tastes in products and opinions about policy priorities are diverse. Consequently, public interest groups cannot be expected to represent all kinds of consumers or to participate in a wide range of regulatory issues where consumer interests are heterogeneous.

Uncertainty. Uncertainty also inhibits the formation of successful interest groups. If the effects of a regulation or the precise identity of the beneficiaries and the losers cannot be predicted beforehand with reasonable accuracy, the incentive to contribute to a lobbying effort is obviously reduced.

In many circumstances uncertainty will be greater about some effects of regulation than about others. If benefits are uncertain but costs are known, advocates of the *status quo ante* will be better represented. In environmental regulation, for example, firms may know very well what different antipollution policies will cost them, but victims of pollution may be considerably less certain of the benefits to themselves of reducing a particular pollutant from a particular source.

A change in rules may create new interest groups. Once the change has occurred, the uncertainty about who will benefit from it is resolved. The large number of potential beneficiaries is transformed into what may be a considerably smaller number of actual beneficiaries. So the change in rules may result in the formation of viable interest groups by eliminating some substantial impediments to their creations.

Since regulators necessarily rely on the range of views expressed by active interest groups in formulating policy, it is important to understand the forces that can produce distortion, bias, and under- or over-representation in that range. Large numbers, the free rider problem, heterogeneity, uncertainty, and unidentifiable interests are all likely to cause some views to go unexpressed. Those who would benefit from the adoption of a particular view may not constitute a viable interest group because the interest itself is too diffuse, ill defined, or uncertain.

The interest group whose views are not heard may even be a group of businesses. Suppose, for example, that deregulation would generate market opportunities for some among a large number of potential competitors. Before deregulation these individual firms may not be able to organize effectively. Those that will ultimately be successful do not yet know who they are because there is uncertainty about which firms will benefit from the change. When the number of potential competitors is large, each firm is likely to see little reason to undertake the cost and risk of contributing to an advocacy campaign.

In the health services industry there is almost certainly an unmet demand for greater pluralism and less homogeneity of service. Viable institutional arrangements might exist, for example, at various points along the continuum from prepaid clinical environments at one extreme to fee-for-service solo practice at the other. Examples include the independent practice association (IPA) and the preferred provider organization (PPO). Until recently, medical establishment interest groups were able to prevent the intermediate options from coming into existence, just as they blocked HMOs for many years. The absence of these hybrid forms from the marketplace means that there are fewer voices advocating reform of the regulations that bar their existence.

Applications to Deregulation Debates

This analysis has predicted what kinds of interest groups are likely or unlikely to be represented in the regulatory and legislative processes. It is useful to examine recent episodes of deregulation to see how well fact accords with theory. We find, as expected, a common theme: consumers are underrepresented. The regulatory authority must be especially careful in assessing how the interests of consumers will be affected by changes in regulation. A second theme: in situations where some small firms and new competitors can be expected to thrive when competitive restraints are removed, their interests are not often heard.

Consider first discount securities brokers. Before deregulation, of course, there were no discount brokers. Undoubtedly many brokers, or people who could easily have qualified to be brokers, were inclined to sell at discount prices if they were allowed to do so. But before deregulation it was very hard to predict which brokers or individuals would increase their market share or successfully enter the market if price competition were permitted. Although some brokers have clearly benefited from deregulation, the twin effects of large numbers and uncertainty explain why such brokers were not an effective interest group before deregulation.

Some consumers were at least indirectly represented in the de-

47

bate over deregulation of brokerage commissions. Recipients of pensions, for example, were represented by the large institutional investors responsible for their pension funds. These financial intermediaries perceived that they would pay lower rates under price competition and lobbied for elimination of price fixing. In contrast, small direct investors were not represented by a lobbying organization.

Consumer interests were, for a long time, perversely represented or not represented at all in the debate over deregulating telephone terminal equipment.[11] The interests of consumers in having a larger selection of higher-quality terminal equipment at lower competitive prices were not adequately represented by independent outside interest groups. Indeed, such consumer interests were represented only by the potential entrants. Deregulation was stalled for a time by the fears of the telephone company and some regulators that local rates would rise and service quality would deteriorate. AT&T and its allies among state regulators were thus able to stall beneficial regulatory reform by focusing attention on a small and chimerical fear: there is no logical basis for concern with local telephone rates as opposed to, say, the overall size of telephone bills, including toll and equipment charges.

A measure of the degree to which deregulation benefited the public can be found in the rapidity with which AT&T customers turned to competitive sources of terminal equipment. AT&T's relative lack of success when faced with competition indicates the extent to which before deregulation it either produced at inefficiently high cost or failed to take advantage of existing technology to produce state-of-the-art products with features consumers wanted. Consumers' actual behavior has revealed their preference for non-AT&T products and has forced changes in AT&T's behavior. But this consumer interest was not well represented by any outside consumer interest group before deregulation.

Consider, as another example, radio station formats. The FCC was ultimately able to deregulate radio format changes as a result of the Supreme Court decision in the *WNCN* case.[12] But in the policy debate and litigation surrounding that decision, radio listeners were not represented according to their actual stake in the outcome. Some public interest lawyers argued for retaining FCC oversight of format changes, as did representatives of listener groups organized to resist changes in the formats of particular stations. Listeners to classical music stations had an interest in opposing deregulation. But quite unrepresented were listener groups that would benefit from format changes. The problem facing such groups was that their members could not identify themselves as such. Although the group whose favorite programs were threatened by change was easy to identify, no one could be sure what the new format or its audience would be. Moreover, to the extent that the change was predictable, the beneficiaries tended to be younger, poorer, and less well educated, whereas listeners to the classical format tended to be the affluent and educated few. Even if the beneficiaries of deregulation could have been identified, they would probably have been much harder to organize.

The interests of consumers were not well represented in the debates over decontrol of energy prices. The so-called public interest groups supported price controls on the grounds that lower prices were better and that energy companies deserved punishment. This position probably did accurately represent the short-term economic interest of some customers. Customer groups that received all the natural gas they wanted at low controlled prices, for example, may have been net beneficiaries of energy price regulation.

The overall effect on consumers, however, was not beneficial. Consumers paid the world price for oil, set by the production and pricing decisions of the OPEC countries. The real effects of regulating domestic oil prices were to subsidize imports and curtail domestic oil and gas production, neither of which had been intended by the policy makers and both of which clearly disserved the public interest. In addition, some producer groups (small refiners) benefited from the way in which price regulation was administered. Small refiners became a vocal and effective interest group in opposition to deregulation.

Consumer interest groups were not very influential in the debate over allowing banks and savings and loans to pay market interest rates to small savers. The large number of small savers creates a free rider problem, and small savers individually have a small stake in the outcome of the debate. They are thus deterred in at least two ways from forming an effective interest group. Individuals with larger amounts to invest usually take advantage of opportunities to earn market rates of interest.

Consumers are similarly underrepresented in debates on the extent and method of regulating environmental quality. Because the costs of pollution controls are passed on in product prices, consumers of manufactured products have a substantial economic stake in environmental regulation. There is obviously a trade-off between the environmental benefits of pollution control and the costs imposed on consumers of manufactured products. But the interests of consumers in this trade-off are not represented, because they are numerous and because their individual interest in particular pollution control regulations is small. Consumers with very strong demands for environmental improvement are represented by environmental groups, but these groups sometimes act in ways contrary to consumer interests because they are not accountable to consumers generally.

Opposition among truckers and railroads to the deregulation of surface freight gradually diminished. Railroads in particular came to believe that regulatory restrictions on prices, entry, and exit worked to their disadvantage. Thus by the end of the deregulation debate railroads and some contract truckers had identified themselves as likely beneficiaries of deregulation and took positions favoring it.

Consumers of freight services were not well represented, and public interest groups were not very active in this debate. Consumers in sparsely populated areas were represented only indirectly. There was the usual political concern over the prices they paid and the service they received. With regard to trucking, this concern was ill founded because no mechanism was identified that would have forced truckers to serve rural communities. Indeed, no general failure of service to rural areas has been identified since deregulation.

Agriculture is very successful in advocating its interests. Agricultural cooperatives administering marketing orders are also successful. They have been able to avoid some of the problems of large numbers and free riders they might be expected to have. Such organizations can obtain complete monopolies on marketing of specific commodities. Moreover, they can deduct their expenses before paying member farmers for the goods marketed. As a result, to the extent that advocacy costs are an allowable expense of the cooperative, the need to solicit voluntary contributions from individual farmers is avoided. An additional advantage of the agricultural industry is that its opponents, consumers, are numerous and thereby underrepresented as usual.

Elimination of anticompetitive regulatory practices in ocean shipping, as well as reduction or elimination of the large subsidies received by that industry, has been blocked by the industry and its unions.[13] I have already discussed some of the reasons why the industry and its unions have been successful in financing their advocacy.

Ocean freight customers, both ultimate individual consumers and shippers, face the familiar problems of large numbers and heterogeneity in organizing their interests. Prospective challengers of the anticompetitive practices of the shipping conferences must also face the fact that foreign governments are even stronger supporters of the conferences than our own. Diplomatic barriers thus reduce the probability of a successful reform effort and therefore the attractiveness of a large-scale advocacy effort.

Conclusion

The interest group model of the regulatory process can be quite successful in explaining some of the phenomena that we observe in the real world, such as interest group opposition to procompetitive change. But reform does happen: airlines are deregulated, ineffective and unnecessary FCC rules are repealed, and the government eventually mandates the availability of HMO options. Regulatory reform in the health care industry is glacial—more like communications with its gradual reforms than like airlines, which were suddenly entirely deregulated. Among the reasons why reform does eventually take place is an understanding by policy makers of this very process and a willingness to transcend it.[14]

Notes

1. *The Federalist Papers* (New York: Mentor, 1961), pp. 78–79.
2. Ibid.
3. Cable television regulation is surveyed in Bruce M. Owen, "The Rise and Fall of Cable Television Regulation," in Leonard W. Weiss and Michael W. Klass, eds., *Case Studies in Regulation* (Boston: Little, Brown, 1981).
4. For a discussion, see Jack A. Meyer, *Passing the Health Care Buck: Who Pays the Hidden Cost?* (Washington, D.C.: American Enterprise Institute, 1983), chap. 2.
5. Deregulation of securities brokers' commission rates is discussed in Hans Stoll, "Revolution in the Regulation of Securities Markets," in Weiss and Klass, *Case Studies in Regulation*; William F. Baxter, "NYSE Fixed Commission Rates: A Private Cartel Goes Public," *Stanford Law Review*, vol. 22 (1970), p. 675; and Lawrence G. Goldberg and Lawrence J. White, eds., *The Deregulation of the Banking and Securities Industries* (Lexington, Mass.: D. C. Heath, 1979).
6. A history of technological change, regulation, and dominant firm strategy in intercity telecommunications is presented in Gerald Brock, *The Telecommunications Industry: The Dynamics of Market Structure* (Cambridge, Mass.: Harvard University Press, 1981), pp. 170–233, 254–86.
7. The Consumer Product Safety Commission's bicycle safety standard is discussed in Nina Cornell, Roger Noll, and Barry Weingast, "Safety Regulation," in Henry Owen and Charles Schultze, eds., *Setting National Priorities* (Washington, D.C.: Brookings Institution, 1976).
8. Clark C. Havighurst, "Decentralizing Decision Making," in Jack A. Meyer, ed., *Market Reforms in Health Care* (Washington, D.C.: American Enterprise Institute, 1983).
9. For a discussion of scope-of-practice limitations, see Rosemary Gibson

and John B. Reiss, "Health Care Delivery and Financing," in Meyer, *Market Reforms in Health Care*.

10. The free rider problem is discussed in Mancur Olson, *The Logic of Collective Action* (Cambridge, Mass.: Harvard University Press, 1965).

11. Deregulation of the telephone customer equipment business is discussed in Brock, *The Telecommunications Industry*, pp. 234–53, and in a majority staff report of the Subcommittee on Telecommunications of the House Committee on Energy and Commerce, "Telecommunications in Transition" (1981), pp. 184–94. See also the two major opinions of U.S. District Court Judge Harold Green in United States v. AT&T, 524 F. Supp. 1336, 1348–52 (1981), and 43 Antitrust and Trade Regulation Report S-1, S-58 (1982).

12. The Supreme Court decision permitting FCC deregulation of radio station format changes is FCC v. WNCN Listeners' Guild, 450 U.S. 582 (1981). The FCC decision to deregulate radio more generally is reported in the *Federal Register*, vol. 46 (February 24, 1981), p. 13888.

13. Maritime regulation is covered by Gerald Jantscher, *Bread upon the Waters: Federal Aids to the Maritime Industry* (Washington, D.C.: Brookings Institution, 1975), and Robert Larner, "Public Policy in the Ocean Freight Industry," in Almarin Phillips, ed., *Promoting Competition in Regulated Markets* (Washington, D.C.: Brookings Institution, 1975).

14. For a more extensive discussion of why reform does take place, see Roger G. Noll and Bruce M. Owen, "What Makes Reform Happen?" *Regulation* (March/April 1983).

4

Reform of the Individual Income Tax: Effects on Tax Preferences for Medical Care

Cynthia Francis Gensheimer

The exclusion of employer-provided medical insurance premiums from employees' taxable incomes might be cut back as part of an effort to introduce more competition into medical care. Employees would then probably purchase less comprehensive health insurance coverage, shoulder more of the cost of their care, and thereby be more cost-conscious consumers. The employer exclusion might be cut back as part of a separate effort to reform the income tax, however, as discussed in this chapter.[1]

Under a comprehensive income tax, for example, employees would be taxed on the value of employer-provided health and accident insurance; they would no longer be able to deduct charitable contributions to nonprofit medical institutions or large out-of-pocket medical expenses; and they would be taxed on the interest on what are now tax-exempt hospital bonds. This chapter discusses how these tax preferences fit into the debate concerning reform of the individual income tax and focuses particularly on the largest tax preference for medical care—the exclusion of employer-provided health insurance.[2]

Current Law and Historical Background

Under a truly comprehensive income tax, individuals would be taxed on all compensation, whether cash or fringe benefits, and all other income, less the associated expenses of earning the income.[3] Much income is now sheltered from taxation through special tax deductions, exclusions, exemptions, and tax credits—called tax preferences.

From its inception in 1913, the individual income tax has never been truly comprehensive, but distortions caused by tax preferences were initially mild, since until World War II the tax applied to a small percentage of the population (under 10 percent) and yielded less than 2 percent of personal income.[4] After World War II the tax yielded much more revenue (annually between 7 and 12 percent of personal income), and its influence over economic decision making grew.[5] In 1947 about 13 percent of personal income was sheltered from individual income taxation through the use of special tax exclusions, itemized deductions, and tax credits; in 1979 about 33 percent of income was so sheltered.[6] The number of provisions granting special individual or corporate tax relief increased from 50 in 1967 to 104 in 1982.[7]

The proliferation of tax preferences for medical care and the increased use of existing preferences follow the same general pattern. Employers' contributions for employees' health insurance were never considered taxable, but no formal statute or ruling addressed the issue until a 1943 ruling of the Internal Revenue Service (IRS) explicitly excluded employers' contributions to group health insurance policies.[8] In 1953 the IRS ruled that employees be taxed on employers' contributions to individual health insurance policies. In 1954, to make the tax treatment of employers' contributions to group and individual plans uniform, the Congress enacted section 106 of the Internal Revenue Code, excluding from tax employers' contributions to all health insurance plans.

Although few employees paid income tax in 1913 and few were covered by health insurance policies supplied by their employers, the growth of the income tax and of health insurance coverage has made the employer exclusion one of the largest tax preferences. Its cost to the federal government in forgone revenue is estimated at $20.2 billion for fiscal year 1985.[9] (The only fringe benefit that costs more in forgone revenue is the exclusion of pension contributions and earnings.)

American companies are concerned, too, about the amount they are spending on health insurance. In 1983 the Chamber of Commerce expected companies to pay $2,000 for each employee for health care— 11 percent of payroll. This amount was $1,250—9 percent of payroll— in 1977.[10] In 1959 companies paid only 2.3 percent of payroll for medical, dental, and life insurance premiums and death benefits combined.[11] According to one set of projections, all employee benefits are expected to rise from 16.5 percent of total compensation in 1983 to between 23 and 39 percent of compensation in 2060.[12]

Between 1960 and 1980 inflation-induced bracket creep pushed many taxpayers into higher tax brackets and thus increased the attractiveness of tax-free fringe benefits. Consider an employee faced with the choice between a $100 cash raise and additional health insurance coverage costing the employer $100 but valued by the employee at $60. At a marginal tax rate of 30 percent, the employee would choose the cash, which would yield him $70 after tax.[13] At a marginal tax rate of 50 percent, however, the employee would choose the additional health insurance coverage, which he values at $60, since he would get only $50 additional cash after tax.

Thus the rapid rise in fringe benefits between 1960 and 1980 may have been a response, in part, to the rising marginal tax rates on cash compensation. A study that attempted to explain the recent rise in the use of fringe benefits determined that a 10 percent increase in marginal tax rates would increase the percentage of compensation paid in the form of health insurance premiums by 4.1 percent.[14]

Interest in Comprehensive Income Taxation

Although persuasive arguments can be made in favor of each tax preference, taken together they have made the income tax complex and contributed to the perception that it is unfair and that tax evasion is on the rise. Because so much income is effectively untaxed, tax rates must be high on the income that remains subject to tax, and high marginal tax rates magnify the distortionary effects of the tax. In general, there is a concern about the tax's effects on work effort, personal saving, and the allocation of investment funds.

These complaints have generated interest in wholesale revision of the individual income tax. Many tax reform bills have been introduced in Congress, most of which call for repeal of all or most tax preferences and reduction of tax rates to one flat rate (hence the name "flat tax") or to a lower set of graduated rates. This approach is called broadening the base of the tax and reducing tax rates, and the resulting tax is called a comprehensive income tax.

The concept of a comprehensive income tax holds wide appeal. Sixty-two percent of the public favor an income tax with a flat rate of 14 percent and very few deductions although when polled on specific tax deductions, a majority advocated retaining most of the larger deductions.[15] Eighty percent favored retaining the deduction for large medical expenses, for instance.[16] The next three sections evaluate the move to a comprehensive income tax by the three standard criteria used to evaluate taxes: equity, efficiency, and simplicity. The revenue raised by repealing tax preferences is assumed to be used to reduce tax rates, so that the yield of the tax would remain unchanged.

Equity

Many people judge the current income tax to be unfair according to both standards of equity: whether equal amounts of tax are collected from individuals in the same economic position and whether the tax appropriately distinguishes among individuals of different economic status.

Like Treatment of Equals. Individuals with equal incomes now pay widely different amounts of tax that depend on their ability and willingness to take advantage of tax preferences. Those with compensation packages composed heavily of fringe benefits, such as employer-provided health insurance, pay less tax than those of equal economic incomes composed of more cash. Since fringe benefits vary with industry, unionization, size of company, and whether workers are full-time or part-time employees or are self-employed, tax rates also vary with those characteristics.

Similarly, individuals of equal incomes pay different amounts of tax that depend on how they spend their incomes. Those who make large charitable contributions, for instance, to nonprofit medical institutions, or who spend large amounts of nonreimbursed medical expenses pay less tax than others of equal income who spend less on tax-deductible items.

Enactment of a comprehensive income tax would make the tax fairer, since repeal of tax preferences would ensure that those of equal income paid the same amount of tax. Many of the preferences, however, such as the deduction for large out-of-pocket medical expenses, were designed to aid persons experiencing hardship, and their repeal could be considered inequitable.

Progressivity. Most people believe that those with the highest incomes avoid paying their fair share of tax because they are best able to use tax preferences. In fact, although those with the highest incomes derive nearly all the benefit from certain tax preferences, low-income taxpayers derive nearly all the benefit from others. Taxpayers with incomes above $50,000, for example, derive most of the benefit from the tax exemption of interest on state and local bonds and from the deduction of charitable contributions. Taxpayers with incomes between $20,000 and $50,000 derive most of the benefit from the deduction for large medical expenses and from the exclusion of employer-provided health insurance, and those with incomes below $15,000 derive nearly all the benefit from the exclusion of disability pay (see table 4–1).

Broadening the tax base. Comprehensive broadening of the tax base would raise additional revenue without significantly changing the distribution of tax liabilities by income class. One study compared the

TABLE 4-1

FEDERAL INCOME TAX REVENUE LOSS FROM SELECTED TAX
PREFERENCES FOR MEDICAL CARE, BY ADJUSTED GROSS INCOME CLASS,
1982 LAW AND 1981 INCOMES

(in millions of dollars)

Adjusted Gross Income Class	Deductibility of Medical Expenses	Exclusion of Employers' Contributions for Medical Insurance Premiums and Medical Care	Exclusion of Disability Pay[a]
Less than $10,000	85	888	127
$10,000–$15,000	190	1,191	22
$15,000–$20,000	299	1,464	1
$20,000–$30,000	827	3,851	3
$30,000–$50,000	1,201	4,470	—
$50,000–$100,000	614	1,450	—
$100,000–$200,000	150	252	—
$200,000 and over	56	53	—
Total[b]	3,422	13,619	153

NOTE: These are losses in federal income tax only and thus do not include losses in social security tax or state income tax. —Means less than 0.5.

a. Beginning in 1985, disability pay will no longer be excluded from taxable income. It will qualify for a tax credit.

b. For fiscal year 1985, the total revenue losses are expected to be $3.410 billion for the deductibility of medical expenses and $20.165 billion for the exclusion of employers' contributions for medical insurance (Joint Committee on Taxation, "Estimates of Federal Tax Expenditures for Fiscal Years 1984–1989," p. 14).

SOURCE: Department of the Treasury, Office of Tax Analysis, September 23, 1982.

distribution of tax liabilities under the 1976 income tax with that under a fairly comprehensive tax base with the same tax rates. Of the additional revenue collected from broadening the tax base in this way but leaving rates unchanged, 18 percent would be paid by those with incomes below $15,000, 56 percent by those with incomes between $15,000 and $50,000, and 26 percent by those with incomes above $50,000.[17] The distribution of total tax paid under 1976 tax law for the same income groups was 11, 59, and 30 percent respectively.[18]

Reducing tax rates. With a more comprehensive tax base, current revenues could be raised with any of a number of lower tax rate schedules, designed to achieve any desired degree of progressivity. A flat-rate tax is, of course, less progressive than a graduated-rate tax with the same personal exemptions.

Efficiency

The efficiency of a tax is gauged by the degree to which it distorts decisions concerning work, saving, and investment.

Broadening the Tax Base. Repeal of tax preferences would encourage investment funds to flow to their most productive uses, as measured by the highest pretax rates of return, instead of toward areas now subsidized through the tax code. Repeal of the tax exemption of interest on bonds for hospital construction, for instance, would end the diversion to hospital construction of funds that could be invested more productively elsewhere. Repeal of all tax incentives for saving and investment might, however, decrease private saving.

Repeal of tax preferences for fringe benefits would lead employers to substitute cash compensation for some fringe benefits. They would probably continue to provide some fringe benefits, possibly including those, like group health insurance, that cost employers less than they would cost employees if purchased independently and those, like provision of exercise facilities, that employers would consider a good investment aside from tax considerations.

Repeal of tax preferences would enable taxpayers to realign their spending patterns to attain maximum satisfaction. One study predicted that expenditures on health insurance would drop by about $7.5 billion annually shortly after repeal of the employer exclusion and might eventually drop by as much as $16.7 billion once all adjustments to the change had been made. (These figures are based on annual expenditures on health insurance premiums of $100.6 billion—the estimate for 1983.)[19] The largest cuts would be made by those in the highest tax brackets, whose insurance is now in effect most heavily subsidized.[20] (A taxpayer in the 50 percent tax bracket saves fifty cents in tax for each $1 of health insurance premiums provided by his employer, while a taxpayer in the 12 percent bracket saves only twelve cents.)

Reducing Tax Rates. If a new set of graduated tax rates were imposed under a comprehensive income tax, rates could be reduced enough across the board that most taxpayers would face lower marginal tax rates. Under a flat-rate tax, high-income taxpayers would face a much lower marginal tax rate (about 20 percent, compared with up to 50 percent now), while the marginal rates of some middle-income taxpayers would rise by a few percentage points.

High marginal tax rates probably cause taxpayers to work and save less and to invest with more consideration of tax consequences. Tax rate reduction would increase the participation of second earners (usually married women) in the labor force and eventually induce married men also to seek longer work hours and more demanding and highly paid jobs and to delay retirement. Although most evidence suggests that saving rates increase only slightly in response to cuts in tax rates, tax rate reduction would improve the allocation of existing investment resources, even if not all tax preferences were repealed. A taxpayer might elect cosmetic surgery, for instance, if his costs qualified for a 70 percent tax deduction but decide to invest in stocks and bonds instead if his tax rate was only 40 percent.

Simplicity

Broadening the Tax Base. In some respects, broadening the base of the individual income tax would simplify the tax, make compliance easier, and reduce the amount of tax planning. Repeal of the deduction for large medical expenses, for example, would eliminate the need for taxpayers to familiarize themselves with the provision and to keep records of out-of-pocket medical expenses.

Some individuals who now owe no tax, however, would be brought into the tax system upon repeal of tax preferences, such as the exclusions of disability pay and social security benefits, that primarily benefit low-income people. Moreover, taxing income, such as that from some fringe benefits, that is not now taxed might present difficult administrative problems and increase the burden of enforcing the payment of the tax.

Fringe benefits. Taxing fringe benefits requires assigning a value to them. Possible approaches to valuation include fair market value, the employer's cost of providing the benefit, and the subjective value assigned to the benefit by the employee. As a practical matter, subjective valuation is not feasible for income taxation, and basing value on the cost to employers of providing benefits would lead to unequal taxation of the same benefit, depending on the employer and his cost. Under a comprehensive income tax employees would generally be taxed on the fair market value of fringe benefits, less, of course, any payment made by the employee for the benefit.

As an example of possible approaches to valuation, consider standby airline trips provided free to airline employees.[21] An employee could be taxed on the value that he assigns to the trip, on the minimal cost to the airline of providing it, or on its fair market value. Fair market value would be difficult to determine, since there is no established market for standby seats. One approach is to dictate in the tax law that the value of a standby seat is some fixed percentage of the price of a reserved seat.[22]

For employer-provided health insurance, the IRS could furnish tables indicating the fair market value of an employee's insurance coverage—the amount that the employee would have to pay to purchase the coverage. The tables would necessarily be very complicated, since there are so many variations in insurance coverage—in deductibles, coinsurance rates, services covered, duration of benefits, and so forth.

A simpler approach, but one that violates the general rule of taxing on the basis of fair market value, is to allocate among the employees the employer's cost of insuring the group.[23] Employers that self-insure would, of course, have to break down the costs of doing so.

The health insurance example illustrates that broadening the base of the income tax and eliminating preferences would not necessarily simplify the tax. It illustrates also the trade-offs between equity and simplicity in taxation.

Reducing Tax Rates. How marginal tax rates were reduced when a comprehensive income tax was enacted would determine whether the rate reduction led to a simpler tax. A flat-rate tax would, for instance, be simpler than the current graduated rate tax, and any reduction in the progressivity of the tax would simplify it.

Under a flat-rate tax, there would be no inflation-induced bracket creep (aside from the relatively small amount caused by the personal exemption), and the tax could be made marriage neutral—so that a couple's tax liability would not change with marriage or divorce. Under a flat-rate tax, taxpayers would engage in much less manipulation aimed at having income taxed in low brackets—after retirement or two children, for example. (Retention of a personal exemption would continue to make a limited amount of this kind of manipulation profitable.)

A flat-rate tax would also make possible some gains in administration. Under a flat-rate tax with no personal deductions, exemptions, exclusions, or credits, nearly all tax could be collected at the source of the income. Financial institutions could accurately withhold taxes on interest and dividends, and employers could withhold tax on all compensation—cash and fringe benefits—provided that fringe benefits were taxed on the basis of their cost to the employer rather than at fair market value.

If the single tax rate were 20 percent, for example, employers would withhold 20 percent of all salaries paid in cash and also 20 percent of the amount spent on fringe benefits. The average taxpayer would then simply file a form annually with the IRS for refund of any personal exemptions allowed by law. The lowest-income taxpayers might find difficulty, however, in waiting until the year's end for refund of their personal exemptions, and exempting them from withholding would probably prove too complicated to be feasible. If corporate and individual income was taxed at the same flat rate, full taxation of fringe benefits for employees of companies paying the corporate tax could be accomplished by disallowing deductions by employers of the costs of providing fringe benefits.

Remaining Problems

Business or Personal Expense? Although employees should not be taxed on fringe benefits provided exclusively for the benefit of their employers, there is necessarily a gray area between services for the benefit of the employer and those for the benefit of the employee. Employer-provided exercise facilities and health-care units, which serve both employers and employees by maintaining a healthy work force, are fringe benefits that fall into this gray area. Other expenses difficult to classify as strictly business or personal include those for company automobiles and for some travel and entertainment. These problems can be particularly difficult to resolve for self-employed people, who would under any income tax be allowed to deduct legitimate business expenses but who might find it relatively easy to tailor business expenditures for personal use.

Substitution of Direct Spending for Tax Preferences. To the extent that direct federal spending programs were enacted to replace tax subsidies repealed upon enactment of a comprehensive income tax, many of the gains in equity, simplicity, and efficiency of the new tax might be lost. The tax rate reduction that could be accomplished with base broadening, for instance, would be lessened unless other spending was curtailed or the budget deficit increased.

Saving and Investment. Although repeal of tax incentives for saving and investment would improve the allocation of funds among investments, problems in taxation of capital income would remain under a

61

comprehensive income tax. Some of the problems, such as double taxation of corporate dividends, could be solved by abolishing the corporate income tax and "integrating" the corporate and individual income taxes.[24] Others could be solved by indexing the income tax fully for inflation.[25] Both measures, however, would be extremely complicated to implement.

Consumption Taxation

Some economists would disapprove of even a fully indexed and integrated income tax, primarily on the basis that it taxes interest twice and discourages saving.[26] They favor a tax on consumption rather than income.

Since income is either spent (consumed) or saved, an income tax with a deduction for saving is a tax on consumption. Under a consumption tax, saving is not discouraged as it is under an income tax, because the aftertax rate of return on saving is the same as the pretax rate of return.[27]

A consumption tax would probably be collected in the same way as the current income tax, with taxpayers reporting their incomes annually. Under a consumption tax, however, they would be allowed to deduct net additions to saving in much the same way as deposits to individual retirement accounts are now treated: contributions are deductible when deposited, but contributions and accumulated earnings are taxed when they are withdrawn.

A comprehensive consumption tax, like a comprehensive income tax, would allow no special deductions, exclusions, exemptions, or credits. Employer-provided fringe benefits, such as medical insurance, would be taxed in full to employees. Some would argue, however, just as they do now for the income tax, that taxpayers be allowed deductions for "nondiscretionary" expenditures on such things as medical care and state and local taxes and for expenditures, such as those for health insurance and education, that further a social goal.

Legislative Proposals

Many bills have been introduced to broaden the base of the individual income tax.[28] Some of them call for one flat rate, others for a lower set of graduated tax rates. The Senate Finance Committee held hearings on broadening the tax base in September 1982 and September 1984, and President Reagan called the flat-rate tax "very tempting."[29]

The bill that has attracted the most attention (S. 1421 and H.R. 3271), originally sponsored by Senator Bill Bradley and Representative

Richard Gephardt, would repeal most special tax preferences but retain some of the more popular ones in limited form. The exclusion for employer-provided health insurance premiums would be repealed, and the deduction for medical expenses would be limited to those exceeding 10 percent of adjusted gross income (as opposed to 5 percent under current law). Interest on general obligation municipal bonds would continue to be exempt from tax, but private hospital bonds would be taxable. The bill would raise the personal exemption and zero-bracket amounts and collapse the tax brackets into four, with a maximum tax rate of 30 percent.

Academic economists have shown the most interest in consumption taxation, although it was endorsed by Martin Feldstein, former chairman of the Council of Economic Advisers, and a bill for a flat-rate tax that closely resembles a consumption tax has been introduced in Congress.[30] The bill (H.R. 5711 and S. 557), sponsored by Representative Richard Shelby and Senator Dennis DeConcini, is modeled on a proposal formulated by economists Robert Hall and Alvin Rabushka. It would require individuals to pay tax on all wages and salaries but not on interest, dividends, or capital gains and would allow no deductions or credits aside from a personal deduction. Businesses would be allowed to deduct all salaries and wages paid in cash but not fringe benefits. Since businesses would pay tax at the same rate as individuals, this provision would amount roughly to a denial of the personal tax exemption of fringe benefits, such as employer-provided health insurance.[31]

Instead of moving immediately to enact a comprehensive income or consumption tax, Congress could take intermediate steps to broaden the income tax base or exclude more saving from taxation. Broadening the base by repealing tax preferences would allow the Congress to raise additional revenue without imposing as many distortions on economic activity as increasing the rates of the tax would. The Tax Equity and Fiscal Responsibility Act of 1982, for instance, cut back several tax preferences, including the medical expense deduction.[32]

Senator Robert Dole, former chairman of the Senate Finance Committee, has suggested that additional revenue could be raised by scaling back tax preferences for fringe benefits.[33] He introduced a bill, S. 640, in the Ninety-eighth Congress that would require employees to pay tax on employers' contributions to health insurance plans exceeding $175 per month for family coverage and $70 per month for individual coverage. The Reagan administration has also proposed caps on tax-free health insurance premiums.

The Deficit Reduction Act of 1984 defined limits on so-called cafeteria plan fringe benefits. Under cafeteria plans, employers allow employees to choose among a variety of tax-free fringe benefits. The most generous plans in essence give employees a budget of tax-free income to spend on a wide variety of employer-provided goods and services. The Treasury Department is concerned that such plans might expand and proliferate, creating inequities, eroding the tax base, and requiring higher rates on income remaining subject to tax.[34] The Deficit Reduction Act of 1984 limits cafeteria plans by specifying that only cash and certain fringe benefits, including employer-provided health insurance, may be offered under them.

Transitional Considerations

Any major tax change would upset financial plans and create large shifts in the wealth and incomes of individuals, businesses, nonprofit institutions, and governments. Values of assets would rise or fall with the change in their tax treatment, and tax liabilities of many individuals would change significantly.

A persuasive case can be made for granting no compensation to those who would suffer from a tax change.[35] The Congress has, however, generally enacted transitional rules to cushion the effects of major changes. It has sometimes grandfathered, or extended old law tax treatment to, transactions entered into before the new law was enacted. In other cases, it has delayed the effective date of a new law to give taxpayers time to adjust to it. (This approach would work well for repeal of employer-provided health insurance, because it would allow time for compensation packages to be renegotiated and redesigned to include more cash and less health insurance.) Since by their very nature transitional rules are complex, delay the beneficial effects of a new law, and often induce taxpayers to engage in unproductive activity to reduce their taxes, they cannot be used to protect taxpayers completely from the adverse effects of a tax change.

Notes

1. For a review of the major proposals for revising the individual income tax, see Congressional Budget Office, *Revising the Individual Income Tax* (July 1983).

2. Health insurance premiums provided by employers are also excluded from the base of the social security tax, but this chapter examines only their exclusion from individual income taxation.

3. Even under the most comprehensive income tax, employers would continue to be allowed to deduct the costs of earning their income. These costs include compensation paid in all forms—cash or fringe benefits. If deductions

for costs of earning income were disallowed, the tax would be a tax on gross receipts, rather than on net income.

4. Richard Goode, *The Individual Income Tax* (Washington, D.C.: Brookings Institution, 1976), pp. 3–4.

5. Department of Commerce, Bureau of Economic Analysis, "The National Income and Product Accounts of the United States," *Survey of Current Business* (September 1981), pp. 73–75, 122–23, and (July 1982), pp. 12, 47.

6. Eugene Steuerle and Michael Hartzmark, "Individual Income Taxation, 1947–1979," *National Tax Journal* (June 1981), pp. 161–62, 165.

7. Congressional Budget Office, *Tax Expenditures: Current Issues and Five-Year Budget Projections for Fiscal Years 1982–1986* (September 1981), p. 8.

8. Congressional Budget Office, *Tax Subsidies for Medical Care: Current Policies and Possible Alternatives* (January 1980), p. 6.

9. Joint Committee on Taxation, "Estimates of Federal Tax Expenditures for Fiscal Years 1984–1989" (November 9, 1984), p. 14.

10. *New York Times*, September 12, 1982.

11. U.S. Chamber of Commerce, *Employee Benefits Historical Data, 1951–1979* (1981), p. 11.

12. Alicia Munnell, "Employee Benefits and the Tax Base," *New England Economic Review* (January/February 1984), p. 44.

13. The marginal tax rate is the percentage of tax collected on a dollar of additional income.

14. James Long and Frank Scott, "The Income Tax and Nonwage Compensation," *Review of Economics and Statistics* (May 1982), p. 216.

15. Harris poll of August 1982, reported in *Business Week*, September 6, 1982, p. 15.

16. Taxpayers are allowed to deduct out-of-pocket medical expenses that exceed 5 percent of adjusted gross income.

17. Joseph Minarik, "The Yield of a Comprehensive Income Tax," in Joseph Pechman, ed., *Comprehensive Income Taxation* (Washington, D.C.: Brookings Institution, 1977), p. 285.

18. Ibid.

19. Amy Taylor and Gail Wilensky, "The Effect of Tax Policies on Expenditures for Private Health Insurance," in Jack A. Meyer, ed., *Market Reforms in Health Care* (Washington, D.C.: American Enterprise Institute, 1983), p. 171.

20. For example, average premiums of those with incomes between $30,000 and $50,000 might eventually decrease by $275 per year if the employer exclusion was repealed, while premiums of those with incomes between $10,000 and $15,000 might decrease by $149 (ibid., p. 172).

21. This example is taken from Joint Committee on Taxation, "Analysis of Proposals Relating to Broadening the Base and Lowering the Rates of the Income Tax" (September 24, 1982), p. 23. In 1921 the IRS ruled that railroad passes given to railroad employees were gifts, rather than income. On the basis of that precedent, airline employees have generally not been taxed on the value of trips provided by their employers. The Deficit Reduction Act of 1984 explicitly excluded from tax the value of fringe benefits such as standby airline flights provided by employers at no substantial additional cost.

22. Testimony of John Chapoton, assistant treasury secretary for tax policy, before the Senate Finance Committee, June 22, 1983, reprinted in *Tax Notes* (June 27, 1983), p. 1193.

23. For group health insurance, this approach can be justified under the fair market value rule on the theory that employees could always band together and purchase group insurance on their own if it was not provided by their employer (Special Committee on Simplification, Section of Taxation, American Bar Association, "Evaluation of the Proposed Model Comprehensive Income Tax," *Tax Lawyer,* 1979, pp. 571-72).

24. For a complete discussion of integration of the corporate and individual income taxes, see Alvin Warren, "The Relation and Integration of Individual and Corporate Income Taxes," *Harvard Law Review* (February 1981), pp. 719-800; and Charles McLure, Jr., *Must Corporate Income Be Taxed Twice?* (Washington, D.C.: Brookings Institution, 1979).

25. For a discussion of indexing capital gains, interest income and expense, depreciation, and costs of goods taken from inventory, see Congressional Budget Office, *Revising the Individual Income Tax,* pp. 67-107.

26. Income is taxed once when it is initially earned, and if a portion of the income is saved and earns interest, the interest is also taxed. This view of double taxation was held by John Stuart Mill, Thomas Hobbes, Alfred Marshall, and Irving Fisher, among others (ibid., p. 110).

27. For an explanation, see ibid., p. 116.

28. For descriptions of some of the bills introduced in the Ninety-eighth Congress, see Joint Committee on Taxation, *Analysis of Proposals Relating to Comprehensive Tax Reform* (September 21, 1984), pp. 39-44.

29. *New York Times,* July 7, 1982.

30. "Why Washington Likes Consumption Taxes," *Business Week,* June 13, 1983, p. 80.

31. So as not to discriminate in favor of those employed by governments and nonprofit institutions that pay no tax, the bill requires those agencies to pay tax on the amount spent on fringe benefits for their employees.

32. Since 1983 only medical expenses exceeding 5 percent of adjusted gross income have been deductible. Formerly, the floor was 3 percent of adjusted gross income.

33. *Tax Notes* (June 27, 1983), p. 1197.

34. Testimony of Chapoton, *Tax Notes,* pp. 1194-96.

35. See Michael Graetz, "Legal Transitions: The Case of Retroactivity in Income Tax Revision," *University of Pennsylvania Law Review* (1977), pp. 47-87.

5

The Determinants of Rising
Health Care Costs:
Some Empirical Assessments

John R. Virts and George W. Wilson

Health care costs have been increasing as a percentage of gross national product (GNP) everywhere in the industrialized Western world.[1] This cost escalation has probably been progressing for centuries by fits and starts. In the United States numerous public policies and programs have contributed to the relatively high escalation experienced in the past several decades. Public and private sector concern is generating a search for diagnosis and prescription. There is no question but that some set of public policies could slow or even halt such escalation, at least for some time—but at what costs and with what other consequences?

The rhetoric concerning the financial problems of U.S. health care has concentrated on the relative rate of health care cost escalation. This concentration is understandable because total costs are among the few easily measurable aspects of health care. The more significant questions to be addressed concern the cost-effectiveness of spending. Unfortunately, cost-effectiveness cannot be readily measured.[2] Health policy analysis will always be of limited value until two fundamental analytical issues are resolved.

First, it must be possible to assess the effects of health care expenditures on the cost of illness—particularly for the nation as a whole but also for communities and individuals. (If this is not possible, we should at least note that the cost of illness has probably declined by more than the increase in expenditure on care, even if the amount of that expenditure may not be economically optimal.)[3] Second, it must be explicitly decided whether cost-effectiveness is to be assessed in relation to individuals or to society.

It is probably fruitless to hope, let alone to expect, that these esoteric issues will be resolved in this century. But because the limitations imposed by the failure to resolve them need to be recognized by policy makers, they must frequently be stated by analysts.

Concentration on the escalation of costs as a policy issue, rather than as a phenomenon to be examined, can misdirect policy. To illustrate, assume that we somehow knew that 10 percent of all spending for health care was due to some form of inefficiency. The complete elimination of such inefficiency would be a clearly desirable goal if it could be achieved at less cost than 10 percent of total health expenditure. Such elimination would not materially affect the escalation of health care spending as a percentage of GNP, however, except during a period of adjustment. Continuing relative escalation of costs would be affected only by influencing some factor that causes unit prices or the number of conditions treated or the resources consumed per treatment to change in relation to the rest of economic activity.

This chapter reports on the use of macroeconomic techniques to identify and estimate the contribution of the proximate causes of the increase of health care costs in the United States from 1965 to 1981. Inflation, demographic trends, rising incomes, the growth of third-party payments, technological changes, and increased government participation are all shown to play a role. In fact, the economic incentives implied by this set of forces are shown to account for essentially all the recent increases in health care costs.

The purpose of this study and its methods are heuristic. The goal is to arrive at the best possible estimates so that public and private policy makers can judge the possible fruitfulness of various policy initiatives and the possible consequences of expecting too much from policy—since, as is shown in the following sections, much of the escalation of costs is a result of general economic conditions and consumers' preferences.

The next section of this chapter reports on empirical conclusions about the relative roles of prices of units of health care goods and services and consumption of those resources in the escalation of expenditures from 1965 to 1981. The extent to which price escalation deviated from what might reasonably have been expected is assessed, given the general inflation experienced during this period. Utilization growth is then examined to establish, roughly, the economic parameters of its behavior. Finally, some recently emerging measures of the concentration of health care spending on families and individuals are followed by conclusions about policies aimed at slowing the escalation of health care costs in relation to GNP.

Cost Escalation, 1965–1981: Prices and Utilization

Total expenditures for health care can be thought of as the arithmetic product of the number of people whose expenditures are being measured (N), the per capita consumption of health care goods and services (U), and the prices of those goods and services (P). Increases in the expenditures of any group—be it the total U.S. population, an employee group, or Medicare enrollees—can stem from increases in any of these factors. The source of actual growth in spending is a beginning point in assessing the meaning of cost escalation for policy purposes.[4]

Widely used and well-accepted methods are available to attribute increases in aggregates such as total U.S. health care spending to increases in the underlying factors of population growth, utilization growth, and price inflation. Table 5–1 shows the results for the period 1965–1981 and for the subperiods 1965–1972 and 1972–1981.

Quite obviously, price inflation has been the major factor in health cost escalation in this country in recent years—especially since 1972. An immediate question is raised: How did the factors P, U, and N work within the various sectors of health care spending (such as hospitals, nursing homes, professional fees)? The summaries in table 5–1 were derived by summing the year-to-year changes reported for the various sectors (see table 5–2).

Data from tables 5–1 and 5–2 reveal, for instance, that the inflation in hospital prices and physicians' fees in the period 1972–1981 ($83.3 billion) accounted for 43.1 percent of the total increase in health care spending ($193.4 billion) during that period. Thus, price inflation clearly needs to be examined—but it needs to be examined for each sector of spending because its effect on cost escalation has been significantly different in various sectors of spending and in different periods.

Imposed versus Specific Price Inflation

Most economists agree that general inflation in the United States during the period 1965–1981 was caused largely or almost entirely by government monetary and fiscal policies, with some additional contribution from structural changes in the U.S. economy, economic shocks, and international events—all causes outside the control of any particular economic sector or industry. The effect of general inflationary pressure on the price changes of a particular sector is referred to here as "imposed inflation."

TABLE 5-1
SOURCES OF CHANGE IN TOTAL HEALTH CARE SPENDING, 1965–1981
(in billions of dollars)

	1965–1981		1965–1972		1972–1981	
	Amount	%	Amount	%	Amount	%
Price inflation	155.6	63.6	23.1	45.0	132.5	68.5
Utilization growth	67.1	27.4	23.5	45.8	43.6	22.5
Population growth	22.0	9.0	4.7	9.2	17.3	9.0
Increased spending	244.7	100.0	51.3	100.0	193.4	100.0

SOURCE: See note 4.

If general inflationary pressure were to have a uniform effect on all sectors, the rate of change in the GNP deflator would be an adequate measure of imposed inflation for any sector. Any sector's specific inflation rate would be the difference between the sector's actual rate of price change and the economywide inflation rate.

Indeed, a common tendency is to compare any economic sector's rate of price change with the economywide average. Divergences from the average inflation rate are then used to make judgments about the performance of producers and markets. The implicit assumption in such simple comparisons of sectoral with economywide inflation rates is that movement to competitive equilibrium rates of return in different production activities should tend to equalize the inflation rates of all sectors. This is not necessarily the case, however. The effects of general inflation will vary widely when sectors differ significantly in labor intensity or the growth in productivity of their factors of production.

Contrast, for example, the production of pharmaceuticals and the typical physician's office or hospital's acute care center. During periods of general inflation the compensation of labor tends to increase at the same rate across the economy, although differences in wages and income tend to persist. Increases in the *cost* of labor, which tend strongly to push up prices, depend on both general inflation and rates of change in labor productivity. Manufacturing activity and service activity have had vastly different productivity histories, as well as different opportunities to increase productivity. In addition, labor costs as a proportion of total costs are inherently higher for services than for manufactured goods.

The authors' previously mentioned paper (note 4) develops a

TABLE 5-2
SOURCES OF CHANGE IN HEALTH CARE SPENDING, BY SECTOR,
1965–1981
(in billions of dollars)

	1965–1981		1965–1972		1972–1981	
	Amount	%	Amount	%	Amount	%
Hospitals						
Price inflation	67.3	64.6	10.1	48.1	57.2	68.8
Utilization growth	28.2	27.1	9.2	43.8	19.0	22.9
Population growth	8.6	8.3	1.7	8.1	6.9	8.3
Physician services						
Price inflation	31.1	67.0	5.0	57.5	26.1	69.4
Utilization growth	11.1	23.9	2.8	32.2	8.2	21.8
Population growth	4.2	9.1	0.9	10.3	3.3	8.8
Dentist services						
Price inflation	9.1	62.8	1.5	53.6	7.6	65.0
Utilization growth	4.0	27.6	1.0	35.7	3.0	25.6
Population growth	1.4	9.6	0.3	10.7	1.1	9.4
Nursing homes						
Price inflation	11.9	53.8	1.8	40.9	10.1	57.1
Utilization growth	8.5	38.5	2.3	52.3	6.2	35.0
Population growth	1.7	7.7	0.3	6.8	1.4	7.9
Drugs and sundries						
Price inflation	9.1	56.2	0.4	9.8	8.7	71.9
Utilization growth	5.2	32.1	3.2	78.0	2.0	16.5
Population growth	1.9	11.7	0.5	12.2	1.4	11.6
Eyeglasses and appliances						
Price inflation	2.5	55.6	0.5	50.0	2.0	57.2
Utilization growth	1.5	33.3	0.4	40.0	1.1	31.4
Population growth	0.5	11.1	0.1	10.0	0.4	11.4
Other[a]						
Price inflation	24.6	66.5	3.8	40.9	20.8	75.1
Utilization growth	8.7	23.5	4.6	49.4	4.1	14.8
Population growth	3.7	10.0	0.9	9.7	2.8	10.1

a. Other professional services, other health services, expense for prepayment and administration, government public health activities, research, and medical facilities construction.

SOURCE: See note 4.

measure of imposed inflation for each health care sector by using the following data: changes in U.S. total private sector average labor compensation; changes in U.S. private sector labor productivity for a relevant broad economic sector, such as all services in the case of hospitals or all manufacturing in the case of eyeglasses and appliances; changes in the GNP deflator as a measure of the change in cost of all nonlabor inputs; and, finally, the labor intensity of each sector.

The estimation of each sector's imposed unit cost inflation—and, thus, imposed price inflation—is then based on three general economic factors: wage escalation, change in labor productivity, and likely nonlabor cost escalation, all measures of aggregate economic performance in many other industries or the entire economy. The final element employed—labor intensity—is derived for each health care sector from data relating to that specific sector. The portion of total inflation of a sector's prices that should be expected to have been imposed by general inflationary forces having thus been accounted for, any difference between actual price inflation and imposed cost inflation is the specific inflation rate of that sector.

The value for policy analysis of estimates of imposed and specific sectoral inflation rates is in helping to assess the effectiveness and possible consequences of initiatives aimed specifically at prices as opposed to initiatives affecting the use or intensity of care. As we have seen, first-round data indicate that "inflation" has been by far the principal cause of the escalation of the national health care bill. Even so, price-control initiatives would make economic sense only if the price inflation were largely specific to health care. Table 5-3, using estimates of year-by-year imposed and specific inflation rates for each health care sector, shows the contribution of specific inflation to total cost increases over the period 1965–1981. Table 5–4 expands the data of table 5-1 to emphasize the relative effects of imposed and specific price inflation.

The total specific inflation of health care prices accounted for 5.52 percent of the change in U.S. health care spending from 1965 to 1981. Specific inflation was responsible for a significantly smaller percentage of annual increases during the 1972–1981 period than during the 1965–1972 period. This observation is consistent with the conventional wisdom that the introduction of Medicare and Medicaid in 1965 led to an immediate increase in relative health care prices but that the effect was moderated during the longer period as adjustments of capacity occurred.[5]

Since the causes of imposed inflation lie outside the control of health care markets and providers, the potential efficacy of price regulation appears to be small. Even if price controls had eliminated all

TABLE 5–3

CONTRIBUTIONS OF SPECIFIC INFLATION TO CHANGES IN HEALTH CARE
SPENDING, 1965–1981
(in billions of dollars)

	1965–1981		1965–1972		1972–1981	
	Amount	%	Amount	%	Amount	%
Hospitals	10.6	4.33	2.8	5.46	7.8	4.03
Physician services	3.1	1.27	1.0	1.95	2.1	1.09
Dentist services	−0.2	−0.08	0.2	0.39	−0.4	−0.21
Nursing homes	0.9	0.37	0.6	1.17	0.3	0.16
Drugs and sundries	−0.9	−0.37	−0.7	−1.36	−0.2	−0.10
Eyeglasses and appliances	0	0	0.3	0.58	−0.3	−0.16
Other[a]	0	0	0	0	0	0
Total	13.5	5.52	4.2	8.19	9.3	4.81

NOTE: Percentage columns show the contribution of specific inflation to changes in total health care expenditure. For example, the $7.8 billion due to hospital-specific inflation in the period 1972–1981 is 4.03 percent of the change in total health care spending during that period ($193.4 billion, as reported in table 5–1).

a. Other professional services, other health services, expense for prepayment and administration, government public health activities, research, and medical facilities construction.

SOURCE: See note 4.

TABLE 5–4

SOURCES OF CHANGE IN TOTAL HEALTH CARE SPENDING, SHOWING
CONTRIBUTIONS OF IMPOSED AND SPECIFIC INFLATION, 1965–1981
(in billions of dollars)

	1965–1981		1965–1972		1972–1981	
	Amount	%	Amount	%	Amount	%
Imposed inflation	142.1	58.1	18.9	36.8	123.2	63.7
Specific inflation	13.5	5.5	4.2	8.2	9.3	4.8
Utilization growth	67.1	27.4	23.5	45.8	43.6	22.5
Population growth	22.0	9.0	4.7	9.2	17.3	9.0
Increased spending	244.7	100.0	51.3	100.0	193.4	100.0

SOURCE: See note 4.

health-care-specific inflation from 1965 to 1981 as estimated here, and had done so with absolutely no direct or indirect social costs, the net benefit to society in 1981 would have been a saving of $13.5 billion (about 5 percent of the $286.6 billion total national health care bill).

The distinction between imposed and specific inflation as defined here provides a first "rough cut" in evaluating the behavior of producers and markets. Since specific inflation may have many causes, however, its sources must be investigated.

The hospital sector has been a primary target for price regulation. Hospital-specific inflation had a greater effect on total health care expenditure than the specific inflation of any other sector, an effect that was especially significant in dollar terms during recent years. Unlike the demand-push cause of specific inflation in the 1965–1972 period, hospital-specific inflation from 1972 to 1981 occurred, in part, for the following reasons:

• Hospital unit labor costs increased at an average annual rate 16.6 percent higher than the benchmark rate used to calculate imposed inflation in the hospital sector. This increase reflects both lower-than-average productivity growth and higher-than-average wage-rate growth.[6] It explains $5.1 billion of the $7.8 billion changes in hospital-sector expenditure due to specific inflation.

• Hospital malpractice insurance premiums increased at an average annual rate four times higher than the rate of increase in the GNP deflator. This increase accounts for $900 million of the expenditure change due to hospital-specific inflation.

• Food and utilities prices paid by hospitals rose at average rates that were 29 percent and 66 percent more rapid than the rate of increase in the GNP deflator. These increases account for $1.0 billion of the change in hospital expenditure.

These three factors explain all but $800 million (about 0.3 percent of the change in total health care spending) of increased hospital expenditure due to specific inflation. Since they lie outside the control of hospital markets and providers, price controls are not likely to produce a substantial social benefit.

Physician-specific inflation, another frequent target of price control policy discussions, accounted for 5.59 percent of the increase in expenditures for physicians and for 1.09 percent of the increase in total health care expenditure during 1972–1981. Some factors that contributed to physician-specific inflation during that period were as follows:

• Although wages of nonphysician employees in physicians' offices increased at about the same rate as the economywide average, the number of employees per physician increased by 24 percent.[7] These two factors accounted for $600 million of increased health care expenditure due to physician-specific inflation. It has been argued that much of the increase in nonphysician personnel has been caused by the growth of clerical workloads created by governmental and private insurance payment systems.

• Malpractice insurance premiums rose much more rapidly than the general price level and accounted for $750 million of the increased expenditure due to physician-specific inflation.[8]

These two elements alone account for all but $750 million of the measured effect of physician-specific inflation during the 1972–1981 period.

The negative values for the effect of specific inflation in three of the sectors indicate that actual inflation rates were below the imposed rates estimated for those sectors. The negative value for drugs and sundries is largely a result of rapid increases in pharmaceutical industry productivity, which increased during 1972–1981 at an average annual rate 44 percent higher than that for all manufacturing and thus moderated increases in unit labor costs.[9] The negative value for dentist-specific inflation is explained, in part, by the increased productivity brought about by the expanded use of dental assistants. There is also some evidence that real returns to dentists fell, in relation to other labor-income returns, during the 1972–1981 period.[10]

Since health care price increases have contributed substantially to rising health care expenditure in recent years, to say that health care price controls would have moderated the rate of increase is tautological. The objective of price regulation, however, should be not a reduction in spending per se but control of price increases that are sector-specific and indicative of economically inefficient behavior by producers.

The study reported here shows that virtually all the medical care price inflation from 1965 to 1981 is accounted for by general inflation, the relative labor intensity of health care production, the behavior of wages during inflation, and the pattern of changes in labor productivity. Applying reasonable data to the health care sector suggests that health care prices have behaved in recent years much as should have been expected, given the general inflationary environment. Therefore, attempts to regulate health care prices do not appear to address either sources or manifestations of inefficiency in health care financing and delivery. Given the potential cost of price controls, it is likely that price regulation in health care would be counterproductive.

In interpreting this conclusion, two characteristics of the analysis must be kept in mind. First, these findings apply to the *rates of change* in health care spending and prices, not to their levels. An alternative form of analysis, probably using subjective value judgments, would be required to formulate conclusions about optimal prices in health care markets. Second, the analytical technique suggested and applied here requires judgment in the selection of some empirical variables. The choices for this study were consciously conservative and tend to overstate the effects of specific inflation (with the possible exception of hospital prices).[11] Another specification might yield somewhat different results, although other reasonable selections would probably not alter the relative magnitudes reported in this paper. Rough sensitivity testing reveals a range of possible error of ± 3 percent in the dollar estimate of the contribution of specific inflation to changes in total health care spending from 1965 to 1981 when other reasonable wage and productivity measures are used to calculate imposed inflation.

This analysis should lay to rest any concern that market power in health care markets is a significant cause of recent price inflation. Had there been a sufficient increase in market power to enable providers to escalate prices significantly beyond increases in costs, this method would have revealed significant unexplained specific inflation. The absence of such evidence removes any reasonable support for health care price controls by those seeking a remedy for perceived market power as a cause of price inflation.

These findings regarding health care do not imply a high degree of economic efficiency in the production and distribution of medical care goods and services or a rejection of any role for employer or public policy in health care. Substantial theoretical and empirical literature, as well as anecdotal information, suggests that significant inefficiency may have occurred because of the excessive use of health care goods and services. This possibility cannot be denied given the data in table 5-1, which show increased use to have been a significant cause of rising health care costs.

Growth in Real Per Capita Utilization of Health Care: Its Contribution to Cost Escalation

Next to be considered is an investigation of the $67.1 billion increase in total U.S. health care costs caused by greater per capita real utilization from 1965 to 1981, shown in table 5-1: $23.5 billion from forces arising during the 1965–1972 period and $43.6 billion from the additional pressures during 1972–1981.[12] Since policy makers are currently focusing on personal health care spending, the analysis requires that the total spending increase be reduced by the real per capita spending growth in four categories of nonpersonal spending: expenses for prepayment and administration, government public health activities, research, and construction of medical facilities. The contribution of additional utilization in these activities to the increase in real total spending from 1965 to 1981 was $7.6 billion ($4.7 billion in 1965–1972 and $2.9 billion in 1972–1981).

The U.S. population aged during the period under study. Older persons consume more health care goods and services per capita than younger persons. Real per capita spending for each of the personal health care sectors by persons both under and over sixty-five in each year, weighted by the proportions of the population in each age group in 1965, can be used to derive estimates of age-adjusted spending. The adjustments for population aging and nonpersonal health care utilization are shown in table 5-5.

The analysis thus far accounts for $190.3 billion of the $244.7 billion increase in the nation's health care costs in the 1965–1981 period. General price inflation, specific health care price inflation, population growth and aging, and increases in nonpersonal spending thus caused nearly 78 percent of the total increase. We now address the $54.4 billion part of the cost escalation caused by increases in age-adjusted utilization of personal care goods and services. This source of increase is larger than total real spending for all health care in 1965 ($41.9 billion).

Real per capita consumption of most goods and services rose in the 1965–1981 period. Productivity rose somewhat; real incomes rose; households, businesses, and governments had more real dollars to spend, and the dollars were spent. The direction of increased spending is heavily influenced, however, by the institutional structure for the production and supply of goods and services, the sorts of markets in which the exchanges for money take place, and the complex matrix of public and private decisions about what is to be sought in markets. We live in a world characterized by individuals seeking scarce resources to consume for a combination of personal and group benefits. The resulting allocation of resources must be evaluated against some sort of standard to test the efficiency of the use of the increased resources consumed by the increased spending. The standard proposed here is, in effect, a historical one only. The question asked is, we are spending much more; does that mean that we are, necessarily, less efficient than we were?

This analysis starts from the assumption that markets differ but that all are influenced to some extent by the forces of income growth, growth in perceived utilities, the relative cost or price of particular

TABLE 5-5

INCREASES IN TOTAL HEALTH CARE SPENDING CAUSED BY GROWTH IN
REAL PER CAPITA AGE-ADJUSTED UTILIZATION OF PERSONAL HEALTH
CARE, 1965–1981

(in billions of dollars)

	1965–1981	1965–1972	1972–1981
Increases caused by total utilization growth[a]	67.1	23.5	43.6
Less:			
Increases in nonpersonal spending	−7.6	−4.7	−2.9
Age adjustment	−5.1	−0.6	−4.5
Increases caused by real per capita age-adjusted personal health care utilization growth	54.4	18.2	36.2

a. From table 5-1.

SOURCE: See note 12.

goods and services, and government activities in the market. In seeking the "right" amount of health care, the consumer faces many costs in addition to prices—for example, queuing, psychic costs, and uncertainty. His or her agents and suppliers of service are not driven by economic forces alone. They are also professionals. The consumer seeks from health care more than just a cure in some hard, objective sense. He or she also looks for a sense of caring and support for his or her sense of worthiness as an individual. Since these elements of cost and benefit from health care are far from new, past relationships of the influence of changes in incomes and relative prices on the demand for health care may be useful in spite of these forces' making health care "different."

This analysis, therefore, assumes that econometric methods can be used to determine the "normal" changes in each sector's age-adjusted real per capita spending to be expected from growth in real consumer income and from the changes in *relative* prices (reductions in spending from relative price increases and increases in spending from relative price decreases). If so, the patterns of spending growth hypothesized from econometrically determined historical income and price responses (elasticities) themselves should be useful. The residuals of unexplained spending growth should also be useful as indicators of the magnitudes of spending growth due to responses to other economic stimuli in health care sectors—the magnitude of spending possibly due to special circumstances, aberrant behavior, or nonmarket forces.

The aggregates of the sources of age-adjusted real per capita increased spending for personal health care for the three periods under study—using econometric estimates of historical responses to changes in real per capita income and relative price changes from different periods—are shown in table 5-6.[13]

All the econometric relations studied (all time periods and all sectors of spending) strongly support the hypothesis that national personal health care spending per capita *does* increase as national income per capita rises and *does* decline as the relative prices of health care goods and services rise, and vice versa. Econometric estimating procedures based on time series data cannot necessarily be expected, however, to yield precise estimates of the response of real per capita age-adjusted consumption to "pure" income and price changes. The results of structural shifts as a consequence of institutional changes (such as the growth of insurance, or prepayment, coverage; Medicare and Medicaid;[14] and public training and construction programs to expand the health care system) will tend to be partly "captured" as societal response to changes in the variables used in the econometric model—income and price. In addition, changes in technology that add to consumers' utility—and perhaps reduce the cost of illness— will shift consumer and societal demand curves. Such effects also influence measured econometric elasticities and residuals.

These various kinds of influence on spending and econometric measures of historical responses to concomitant, measurable changes in income and price varied within the 1929–1981 period for which national income account data are available.[15] Judgment, based on historical perspective, led to a study of the econometric relationships for three historical periods in addition to those for the entire 1929–1981 period less the World War II years. The periods' historical forces at work and consequences for econometric estimation are outlined in table 5-7.

Statistical techniques confirm that the estimates of response of spending to income and price changes from different periods' data are statistically different and thus fail to reject the hypothesis that different forces were at work. Income and price elasticities estimated from data for the periods 1946–1964 and especially 1965–1981 "explain" a very high proportion of the $54.4 billion increase in spending stemming from real per capita age-adjusted consumption for the 1965–1981 period as response to forces paralleling those of income and relative price changes. (Note very low "residual" estimates in table 5-6, sec-

TABLE 5-6
ESTIMATED SOURCES OF INCREASES IN REAL PER CAPITA AGE-ADJUSTED
PERSONAL HEALTH CARE SPENDING, 1965–1981
(in billions of dollars)

	1965–1981	1965–1972	1972–1981
A. Elasticities from data for 1929–1981 less World War II			
Total	54.4	18.2	36.2
Income growth	31.0	12.3	18.7
Relative price increase	−8.4	−2.0	−6.4
Increased third-party payment	20.1	6.8	13.3
Public sector	12.7	4.5	8.2
Private sector	7.4	2.3	5.1
Residual	11.7	1.1	10.6
B. Elasticities from 1929–1941 data			
Total	54.4	18.2	36.2
Income growth	20.5	6.6	13.9
Relative price increase	−13.6	−3.8	−9.8
Increased third-party payment	27.1	10.4	16.7
Public sector	16.9	6.9	10.0
Private sector	10.2	3.5	6.7
Residual	20.4	5.0	15.4
C. Elasticities from 1946–1964 data			
Total	54.4	18.2	36.2
Income growth	35.4	12.8	22.6
Relative price increase	−4.4	−0.9	−3.5
Increased third-party payment	17.4	6.1	11.3
Public sector	11.0	4.0	7.0
Private sector	6.4	2.1	4.3
Residual	6.0	0.2	5.8
D. Elasticities from 1965–1981 data			
Total	54.4	18.2	36.2
Income growth	46.7	15.6	31.1
Relative price increase	−2.1	−0.7	−1.4
Increased third-party payment	8.2	3.0	5.2
Public sector	5.1	2.1	3.0
Private sector	3.1	0.9	2.2
Residual	1.6	0.3	1.3

SOURCE: See note 12.

TABLE 5-7

ECONOMIC CHARACTERISTICS AND ECONOMETRIC CONSEQUENCES OF
THE HEALTH CARE ENVIRONMENT, 1929–1981

Period	Economic Characteristics	*Consequences for Measures of:*	
		Response to income change	Response to relative price change
1929–1941	Little innovation Little third-party payment Little income or supply subsidization	May yield best estimate of income response	May yield best estimate of price response
1946–1964	Strong innovation Growing third-party payment Little income subsidization Growing public programs leading to future expansion (number of professionals; Hill-Burton construction)	May capture results of innovation	May be close to pure response but possibly biased
1965–1981	Strong innovation Growing third-party payment Medicare-Medicaid income subsidies for health care Results of public program expansions of facilities and the number of professionals	May be heavily clouded by innovation *and* income subsidies and supply subsidies	Heavily clouded

SOURCE: Authors.

tions C and D.) This tends to confirm that the time period for data selected to estimate these and other measures is crucial to the usefulness of the estimates, while the analysis immediately above indicates how the time period estimates may be useful to improve on estimates of magnitude for public or private policy analysis. Clearly, however, a substantial element of judgment will enter into any allocation of the

$54.4 billion expenditure increase into estimates of magnitudes from various sources.

The econometric analysis of income and price responses (elasticities) from the 1929–1941 period may offer the best available estimates of these effects without the intrusion (statistically) of hard-to-quantify causes of increased spending (see table 5–7). Table 5–8 summarizes the data from the analyses of inflation effects, population changes, and the authors' best guess of "pure" income growth and relative price change effects based on measures calculated from the 1929–1941 period.[16]

The rate of innovation and technology change in health care in the postwar years clearly was great and almost certainly increased demand for care over what it would otherwise have been. The influence of innovation may statistically appear to have increased the elasticity of demand with respect to income, shifted the demand curve, or both. The advent of public programs to expand health care production capacity would have had a similar effect. These were largely under way in the same 1946–1964 period, but had relatively little effect on personal spending in this period.

The economic forces of technological change continued through the 1965–1981 period, but the use of Medicare and Medicaid to subsidize some incomes and the increased capacity subsidized by public programs additionally cloud the income response measure from this period. The very low residuals resulting from use of response (elasticity) estimates from these recent periods, coupled with the very high statistical significance of the econometric estimates themselves, lend confidence to the belief that some combination of changes in economic variables, behaving in a pattern similar to the measured changes in per capita real incomes and relative prices, is causing changes in age-adjusted utilization. The question for policy purposes, therefore, is one of attempting to account for the changes by source— income, relative price, income subsidization, new technology, and capacity change—more completely than is done in table 5–8.

The data of table 5–8 explicitly leave spending growth due to technological change, subsidization of demand, and subsidization of supply in the residual of $20.4 billion (also shown in table 5–6, section B). The demand curve changes caused by these factors, net of the effect on relative prices, may be estimated from the data in table 5–6. Such estimates will be the differences between the residual estimates (the lower residuals from using data from later periods interpreted as resulting from demand curve change) obtained by using the 1946–1964 or 1965–1981 estimates (table 5–6, sections C and D) of elasticities and the 1929–1941 period estimates. Thus $14.4 billion—1929–1941

TABLE 5-8
SOURCES OF CHANGE IN TOTAL HEALTH CARE SPENDING, INCOME AND
PRICE RESPONSES ESTIMATED FROM 1929–1941 DATA, 1965–1981
(in billions of dollars)

	Amount	Percentage of Total
Total spending increase	244.7	100.0
Price inflation effects	155.6	63.6
Explained by general inflation or other general economic conditions	150.5	61.5
Medicare/Medicaid demand-push, other specific inflation	5.1	2.1
Increased spending for nonpersonal health care (R&D, construction, administrative costs, public health programs)	7.6	3.1
Demographic changes	27.1	11.1
Population growth	22.0	9.0
Population aging	5.1	2.1
Subtotal—forces largely external to health care and not amenable to policy concerning personal health care	190.3	77.8
Changes in per capita utilization of personal health care	54.4	22.2
Growth in real per capita after-tax income	20.5	8.4
Rising relative health care prices	−13.6	−5.6
Increased third-party payment	27.1	11.1
Private sector	10.2	4.2
Public sector	16.9	6.9
Not explained (residual)	20.4	8.3

SOURCE: See note 12.

residual (table 5-6, section B) less 1946–1964 residual (section C)—is an estimate of the contribution to spending growth of technological change (innovation) based on the historical view of major economic forces operating differently in this period.[17] In like manner, $4.4 billion—1946–1964 residual less 1965–1981 residual (sections C and D)—is an estimate of the contribution to spending of the Medicare and Medicaid subsidization of incomes and the greater access created by the subsidization implicit in public programs to increase the supply of health care (number of professionals and Hill-Burton hospital expansion).[18] Table 5-9 illustrates this more detailed breakdown of the residual from the bottom line of table 5-8, with the "unexplained" source of 1965-1981 increased health care costs reduced to the table 5-6, section D, residual of under $2 billion, or less than 1 percent.

It should be *clearly* noted that these estimates of the effects of technological change and subsidization are strictly inferential and judgmental. The statistical techniques applied merely demonstrate that the price and income elasticities estimated from data from the various time periods are not the same and that the differences are unlikely to have been caused by chance alone. It is the economists manipulating the data who have judged that the differences were probably caused by specific forces changing the demand and supply curves for personal health care goods and services. It is also the economists who further judge that, for purposes of policy analysis, the inferential estimates of the effects of technological innovation, and capacity plus income subsidization so derived are useful and possibly the best available.

As used here, technological change includes not just the introduction and diffusion of new equipment (CAT scanners) or new procedures (organ transplants or bypass surgery) but a host of other changes. Among these would be the greater use of nursing homes in place of family care for the aged or infirm, the prophylactic use of antibiotics in some surgeries, the higher skills required (or at least provided) in hospitals, and perhaps even the resources consumed by the practice of so-called defensive medicine. In no way can this analysis demonstrate either the cost-effectiveness or the cost-ineffectiveness of the 5.9 percent of the total increase in health care costs from 1965 to 1981 thus attributed to change in technology. The data do seem to say, however, that even in the absence of significant changes in incomes or the apparent prices of health care, such new technology would have appeared valuable enough to patients and physicians to have substantially increased spending.

On the basis of the responsiveness of real per capita age-adjusted personal health care spending to relative price changes in the 1929–

TABLE 5-9
SOURCES OF THE UNEXPLAINED RESIDUAL FROM ESTIMATES OF CHANGE
IN TOTAL HEALTH CARE SPENDING, 1965-1981
(in billions of dollars)

	Amount	Percentage of Total
Total unexplained residual from table 5-8	20.4	8.3
Changes in technology (innovation)[a]	14.4	5.9
Capacity and income subsidization[a]	4.4	1.8
Not explained (residual)	1.6	0.6

a. Judgmental inference.
SOURCE: See note 12.

1941 period, table 5-8 reveals that about 11.1 percent of the 1965-1981 increase in health care costs was due to increases in third-party payments—particularly because of Medicare and Medicaid. The same basic econometric data indicate, however, that the combined effects of imposed and specific inflation on the prices of health care goods and services in relation to other consumer prices *reduced* national expenditures by about 5.6 percent from what they would otherwise have been.

This pattern of analysis thus indicates two things about real health care spending and the prices for units of health care goods and services. First, as is probably true of all services, unless incomes rise or the relative personal utility of the consumption rises, utilization will have a tendency to decline, since relative prices will tend to increase over time—even without general inflation. Second, halting, slowing, or reversing the increase of third-party payment will slow the rate of escalation of total health care costs.

On average, the responsiveness of real per capita age-adjusted personal health care spending to growth in individuals' real spendable income estimated from 1929-1941 data is slightly less than for the average consumer good. (Economists refer to this response as being "slightly less than unitarily income elastic.") Still, on the basis of these data, 8.4 percent, or $20.5 billion, of the health care cost escalation from 1965 to 1981 would have occurred even if 1929-1941 payment mechanisms and subsidization programs had been in place and only 1964 health care technology had been available.

These same estimates of the sources and contributions of increased expenditures on health care can be used to account for the growth in the proportion of GNP consumed by health care costs. Table 5–10 and figure 5–1 present these results.

This analysis indicates that all but about one and one-third percentage points of the increase from 1965 to 1981 in the proportion of GNP consumed by health care was caused by forces outside the influence of public or private policy concerning personal health care spending. The culprit responsible for about 60 percent of the escalation was the interaction of the labor intensity of health care, inflation-driven wage increases, and the relatively low rate of productivity growth common to most service activities. Even a cessation of general inflation will only slow—not halt—the rise in health care costs as a proportion of GNP unless productivity increases somehow match the average for the entire economy, including manufacturing and agriculture. This is unlikely for service industries; thus the rise in the proportion of GNP consumed is almost certain to continue, although the rate of the recent past will be slowed if general inflation is brought under control. If wages in health care continue to rise more rapidly than in the rest of the economy—whether this be catch-up or not—some of the gain from a lowered rate of general inflation will be lost.

The data indicate that nearly one percentage point of the increase of GNP consumed by health care from 1965 to 1981 was caused by increased third-party payments which reduced prices as seen by consumers. The actual increase in relative prices dissipated some of this rise, however, so that the net effect of relative price movements accounted for slightly less than five-tenths of a percentage point of the rise in GNP proportion. If the proportion of total spending paid for through third-party payers, public and private, should remain stable, this analysis indicates that the rise in the proportion of GNP consumed by health care would be slowed.

New technology, in the broad sense used here, accounted for nearly one-half of one percentage point of the 1965–1981 increase in the proportion of GNP consumed by health care. In a sense, this source of spending growth was partially offset by the less-than-economywide average responsiveness of health care spending to income growth exhibited in the 1929–1941 period and assumed to persist. Clearly, if the rate of development and diffusion of new health care technology is slowed, the rate of increase of spending for health care goods and services will slow.

As is frequently the case, these econometric data leave much to be desired in assurance that the measurements are accurate enough to be useful for policy purposes. Even accepting the data as being heuris-

TABLE 5-10
Sources of Increase in Expenditures on Health Care from 6.1 to 9.8 Percent of GNP, 1965–1981

Total increase in percentage of GNP expended	100.0
Growth in health care prices greater than GNP deflator growth	63.8
Personal health care prices	60.4
Explained by general inflation or other general economic conditions	55.7
Medicare/Medicaid demand-push or other specific inflation	4.7
Nonpersonal health care prices (costs)	3.4
Population aging	4.7
Utilization growth of nonpersonal health care (R&D, construction, administrative costs, public health programs)	4.3
Subtotal—forces largely external to health care and not amenable to policy concerning personal health care	72.8
Changes in per capita utilization of personal health care	27.2
Less than average response to income growth	−4.4
Increase in relative health care prices	−12.7
Decrease in relative price to consumers caused by third-party pay	25.3
Public sector	15.8
Private sector	9.5
Changes in technology (innovation)	13.4
Capacity and income subsidization	4.1
Not explained (residual)	1.5

NOTE: Two examples of the use of these data are as follows. The 9.8 percent of GNP expended for health care in 1981 would have been 8.8 percent (6.1 percent + [3.7 percent × 0.728]) even if per capita utilization had not grown. If the effects of third-party pay, public and private, had not occurred, the percentage of GNP expended would have been reduced to 8.9 percent (9.8 percent − 3.7 percent [0.158 + 0.095]).
SOURCE: See note 12.

tically the best available, they raise such questions as, What were we accomplishing with all that spending? No answer to such questions is possible from these sorts of data. Some additional measures of an entirely different kind, however, bear on such questions. We believe

FIGURE 5-1
CONTRIBUTIONS TO INCREASED PERCENTAGE
OF GNP EXPENDED ON HEALTH CARE, 1965–1981

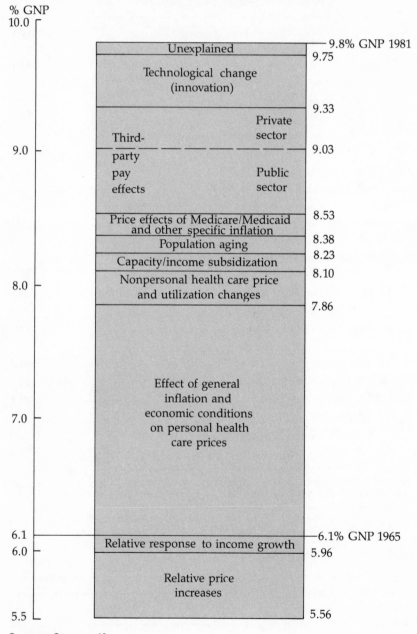

SOURCE: See note 12.

they should be considered in conjunction with this economic analysis of the sources and causes of spending growth in analyzing health care spending for insight into the possible consequences of policy change.

The Concentration of Health Care Spending

Analysts, particularly actuaries, have been aware of the concentration of health care spending in a relatively small part of the population. After all, someone who is not sick spends little on health care. Although going to the hospital is expensive, it is fortunately a rare event for most of us. The phenomenon of concentrated health care spending bears on the nature of health, health care, the current state of the art, and the human condition. Some measurements of the concentration of health costs that have recently received some attention follow.[19]

The Congressional Budget Office reports that in 1978 just 5 percent of the families covered by the federal employees' Blue Cross plans incurred nearly 50 percent of the total bills.[20] In 1979, 7 percent of Medicare enrollees accounted for 67 percent of all Medicare expenditures, and 28 percent of Medicare dollars are spent for people who are in the last year of their lives. Several studies of populations of high users of hospital care confirm these kinds of concentration of costs among relatively small numbers of patients—as well as the dim prognosis for many such patients' conditions.

This concentration of care has been confirmed in private employers' health benefit plans. One company found that, in a recent twelve-month period, 1 percent of the people who filed any claims at all—active employees, retired employees, survivors, or dependents—incurred 26 percent of the total costs of all of those who filed claims.[21] Five percent of the total group incurred about one-half of the total costs—much like the reported federal employee experience—and 10 percent incurred two-thirds of the total costs. Breaking the entire group of beneficiaries into two groups—active employees plus dependents and survivors and retired employees plus dependents—showed the same degrees of concentration in the two groups. The average per capita costs of the younger employee-plus-dependent group were lower, but the concentration of the two groups' spending was essentially the same.

The same company's data was used to examine two additional subjects: the rate of survival of those people who incurred very high health care costs in a twelve-month period and the incidence of people repeating as high spenders in the following year. These data, for all beneficiaries, are summarized in table 5–11. About 25 percent of the high spenders during the first twelve-month period either did not

TABLE 5-11
EXPERIENCE OF HIGH CONSUMERS OF HEALTH CARE
AMONG BENEFICIARIES OF A
PRIVATE EMPLOYER'S HEALTH BENEFIT PLAN, 1981–1983
(percent)

Percentile of Spenders 5/1/81 to 4/30/82	Percentage in Same Spending Percentile 5/1/82 to 4/30/83	Percent Deceased 4/30/83	Percent Either High Spenders or Deceased Following Year
Top 1	12	13	25
Top 5	20	5	25
Top 10	24	3	27

SOURCE: Authors.

survive their illness or were high spenders the next year as well. In the smaller population of survivors, retirees, and their dependents, the proportion who did not survive or who repeated as high spenders rose to nearly 40 percent.

The health care system in this country seems to have evolved toward providing care very, very intensively for a small part of the total population. In addition, the medical prognosis for the recipients of such high-intensity care must frequently be dim.

We are in no sense addressing the "goodness" or "badness" of these facts. We do suggest, however, that public policy makers, business managers, physicians, and hospital administrators must be willing to recognize the implications of these facts more fully. For example, any public or private policy change that affects only the spending of the 90 percent of the population that accounts for one-third of the nation's health care bill is *not* likely to slow the escalation of total national health care costs significantly. These data should, therefore, be considered both in forming expectations of what policy changes can accomplish and in assessing the benefits in relation to the costs of changes.

In many areas of consideration—including, perhaps, those personal and professional areas where actual treatment is considered—there is a need to analyze the effect on the 5 to 10 percent of patients who are such high users of care. Cost constraints of any form, for example, will seemingly have to fall heavily on this relatively small population if they are to affect total national costs. Since the age group over sixty-five, the Medicare population, constituting about 11 percent of the total population, consumes nearly 30 percent of the nation's health care, whatever is done to control Medicare costs is bound to have a serious effect on many individuals in the groups that have been the high users. Policy makers must seriously consider the effect of changes on the trend of increasing life expectancy of the U.S. population at age sixty-five, for example. From the year of Medicare's introduction, 1965, to 1980, life expectancy at age sixty-five increased 1.8 years.

A most important characteristic of the concentration of health care spending, confirmed by empirical evidence, is that the degree of concentration has not changed much, if at all, in recent years.[22] The implication is that the effects of economic forces on spending for health care (incomes, relative price changes, subsidization, technological change) have spread evenly over the spectrum of illnesses or conditions treated. We do not seem to be concentrating resources more heavily on "serious" conditions than in the past. Real per capita age-adjusted spending has apparently increased at about the same rate for the 90 percent of the population accounting for about one-third as for the 10 percent accounting for two-thirds of all spending.

Health Policy Conclusions

It is useful to view our problems of health care costs in the context of history and philosophy even in a discussion of their economics. The 1946–1964 period saw an explosion of growth in our country in virtually all economic areas, accompanied and partially caused by very significant application of new technology to production of all sorts. The great expansion of our use of the "growth dividend" into many sorts of income-redistribution programs led to the beginnings of a heavily mixed public-private economy.

These trends, heavily reinforced in the early part of the 1965–1981 period, ran into the very different economic environment of the 1970s. The growth dividend virtually disappeared. Other priorities arose and continue to arise to lay claim to a resource pool that at times seems stagnant but really is only expanding less rapidly than societal expectations would require. The United States, in common with its international partners and economic competitors, failed to anticipate the clash of expectations with reality, and serious inflation was generated, which has compounded the basic problems. The country's belated efforts to eliminate inflation caused additional short-term reductions in resource generation, not only eliminating any growth dividend, but also bringing about a real decline.

All services began to grow in relation to goods in the 1965–1981 period—and, on average, the services' increased penetration into

GNP was fed by the same interaction among wage rates, labor intensity, and relative labor productivity described above as driving up health care costs and relative prices. The effects of this phenomenon on the interpretation of data on the magnitude of the structural shift to consumption of services rather than goods is worthy of further study.

Most democracies have been struggling to fulfill their electorates' desires to implement in some measure individuals' "right" to health care. In the 1946–1981 period, the United States responded in typical fashion to the forces that led to national health insurance (NHI) in other countries. With the addition in 1966 of Medicare and Medicaid, a set of diverse institutions, centralized and decentralized, now exists to answer individuals' needs and desires—including charity and welfare care and employment-based insurance. It is financed by progressive income taxation, payroll taxation, property taxation, gross income taxation, and, at least implicitly, sales and excise taxation. Questions of equity and the incidence of cost differ in the United States from those in countries with other programs. For many analytical purposes, however, our current system of health care delivery and financing should be considered one form of NHI. It suffers from the same economic and philosophical problems as any form of NHI, including problems of equity and affordability.

This economic analysis leads to the following conclusions for consideration by other disciplines, policy analysts, and policy makers. That part of the recent escalation of U.S. health care costs that could have been eliminated simply by managing costs better while the same number of people were treated for the same conditions is far less than the conventional wisdom seems to suggest. Moreover, significant changes in current institutional structures that actually slow the escalation of costs will almost certainly be accompanied by adverse effects, first, on the care being received by the 5 to 10 percent of the population now receiving one-half to two-thirds of the care delivered and, second, on R&D, innovation, and technological change, which many consider as important a part of our health care system as the delivery of care itself.

This analysis is not meant to imply that today's system is economically efficient or that changes are not desirable and possible. What must be weighed are the costs and benefits of the alternative structures for delivery and financing implied by policy initiatives. The present public and private policy agenda of stimulating consumers' financial incentives through increased sharing of premium payments, deductibles, and copayments along with greater awareness of individual responsibility for health and the care sought seems to be in the correct direction. Efforts by broad-based local coalitions of interested parties to achieve a rational allocation of resources are also potentially effective. These forces all tend toward the needed oversight and review of resource utilization necessary for accountability and understanding. Patients, attending physicians, administrators, and payers are becoming, as they must, increasingly involved in the assessment of all levels of cost-effectiveness: individual case, institution, and community.

When the issues of health care cost escalation are put in context, the need for massive restructuring of our system of finance and delivery systems seems to disappear. Moreover, the damage that might be done by sharp cutbacks in spending could be significant. The evolution of reforms in the financing system that bring the cost of care more directly to consumers' attention should continue. As these incremental reforms unfold, complex problems of ethics and philosophy will emerge. We will face the tough trade-off between the cost of care and the quality and availability of care. Our results show that notions of massive waste in the system that can be eliminated to provide large savings are mistaken. Quick "solutions" are likely to prove to be illusions. Instead, we must gradually evolve policy reforms that address the fat that *does* exist in the system while preserving the spending increases needed and desired by the population.

Notes

1. Robert J. Maxwell, *Health and Wealth* (Lexington, Mass.: Lexington Books, 1981).

2. U.S. Congress, Office of Technology Assessment, *Health Technology Case Study 24: Variations in Hospital Length of Stay: Their Relationship to Health Outcomes*, OTA-HCS-23 (Washington, D.C., August 1983).

3. Jack Hadley, *More Medical Care, Better Health?* (Washington, D.C.: Urban Institute Press, 1982).

4. Data and analysis for this and the following section are taken from John R. Virts and George W. Wilson, "Inflation and the Behavior of Sectoral Prices," *Business Economics*, vol. 18, no. 3 (May 1983), pp. 45–54. See this article and its references for data and methods used.

5. The authors' judgment is that the $4.2 billion contribution to increases in health care spending from 1965 to 1981 occurring in the 1965–1972 period was an economically "normal" price-rationing response to the increased real demand generated by the Medicare and Medicaid programs, when supply was relatively fixed.

6. Although hospital wages rose relatively rapidly, available evidence suggests that they have been, and perhaps still are, below the economywide average for similar skills. See, for example, Health Care Financing Administration, "Employment, Hours, and Earnings in the Private Health Care Sector," *Health Care Financing Trends* (June 1982).

7. Merian Kirchner, "Non-Surgical Practice: What's the Key to Higher Earnings?" *Medical Economics* (February 1981), p. 197.

8. Health Care Financing Administration, *Issues in Physician Reimbursement* (Washington, D.C., 1981).

9. U.S. Bureau of Labor Statistics, *Handbook of Labor Statistics* (Washington, D.C., 1981).

10. Paul Feldstein, "A Review of Productivity in Dentistry," in John Rafferty, ed., *Health Manpower and Productivity* (Lexington, Mass.: Lexington Books, 1974); and Barry H. Waldman, "The Reaction of the Dental Profession to Changes in the 1970's," *American Journal of Public Health* (June 1980), pp. 619-24.

11. The CPI component for hospital services is thought to overstate price changes because it understates qualitative changes in service. Data here are based on the national hospital input price index. Use of the CPI component would indicate, for the 1972-1981 period, $7.5 billion additional specific price inflation and an identical reduction in increased utilization.

12. The analysis and results reported here are taken from a working paper in progress: George W. Wilson and John R. Virts, "Rising Health Care Utilization: An Empirical Investigation." Data and analysis for only the 1965 to 1981 period are reported here. However, preliminary analysis of data through 1983 indicates only marginal changes in the percentage distribution of the causes of increased spending from that reported here. None of our conclusions has been changed by analysis of additional data.

13. Income and price elasticities were estimated for each sector of spending (hospital, physician, etc.), using available data from the periods 1929-1941, 1946-1964, 1965-1981, and 1929-1981 less the World War II years. The econometric procedure employed a simultaneous seven-sector demand model. The model was estimated using a Zellner regression technique similar to three-stage least squares. These elasticities were then used, sector by sector, to estimate "normal" spending increases, which were aggregated for estimates of the effect on total personal spending.

14. Medicare and Medicaid should be viewed as having two economic effects. First, they serve, like other third-party-payment programs, to reduce the apparent price of health care to the consumer. Second, they subsidize the consumer's income.

15. The period 1942 through 1945 was eliminated in these studies because of the influence of World War II on all spending patterns.

16. The usefulness of income and price elasticities calculated from the 1929-1941 period data is supported by an alternative econometric procedure also employed in this study. Data from the entire 1929-1981 period (less the World War II years), including so-called dummy variables representing the various periods themselves (that is, 1929-1941, 1946-1964, and 1965-1981), were used to derive additional estimates of the elasticities, employing the econometric technique noted earlier. The dummy variables were added to account for shifts in the demand curves due to different economic and political conditions thought to have existed during each subperiod. The dummy variables pick up the effect of such demand shifts on the elasticity estimates.

They therefore provide a measure of the magnitude and statistical significance of changes in the price and income elasticities across the subperiods. The causes of the changes are not revealed by the methodology but must be based on the knowledge and judgments of the policy analyst. This dummy variable procedure indicated the following results: (1) relatively large and statistically significant shifts in price and income elasticities were observed in the hospital, physician, drug, and nursing home sectors and related, as expected, to the recent subperiods. (2) Much smaller variations, some of which were not statistically significant, were observed for price and income elasticities in the dental and eyeglasses/appliances sectors. The price and income elasticities estimated by this procedure from data for the entire 1929–1981 period are statistically equivalent to those estimated from 1929–1941 data.

17. Three critical assumptions are required for this inference. First, it must be assumed that innovation, as broadly defined in this chapter, was the only significant factor that shifted the demand curve during the 1946–1964 period. Second, it must be assumed that innovation progressed during that period in a consistent pattern with respect to changes in incomes and relative health care prices. Third, it must be assumed that the pattern of actual innovation, in relation to changes in incomes and prices, was the same in the 1946–1964 and 1965–1981 periods. If these assumptions are correct, the estimated elasticities for the period 1946–1964 would capture the total effect of price, income, *and* innovation. The heuristic method employed here is to take the difference between the explained variation in 1965–1981 spending when all three effects are thought to be captured (that is, using the 1946–1964 elasticity set) and the explained variation in 1965–1981 spending when only the price and income effects are thought to be captured (that is, the 1929–1941 elasticity set) as an estimate of the effect of innovation on spending.

18. The assumptions described in note 17 are required for this inference as well. It is further assumed that during the 1965–1981 period, in addition to the consistent influences of price, income, and innovation measured by earlier periods' data, demand was influenced by government programs that subsidized access to and availability of health care markets and services. These additional influences are assumed to be captured by the 1965–1981 elasticity set and thus to cause the observed increase in statistically explained variation in 1965–1981 spending, in relation to that resulting from use of the 1946–1964 elasticity set.

19. See also Frank A. Sloan, "The High Cost of High-Cost Illness: Description and Policy Alternatives" (unpublished manuscript, Department of Economics, Vanderbilt University, Nashville, Tennessee).

20. U.S. Congress, Congressional Budget Office, *Catastrophic Medical Expenses: Patterns in the Non-elderly, Non-poor Population,* December 1982, p. xviii.

21. Since potential beneficiaries who had no claims at all in the period studied are not included, the degree of concentration of spending is understated.

22. Sloan, "High Cost of High-Cost Illness"; and Ronald Anderson et al., *Expenditures for Personal Health Services: National Trends and Variations, 1953–1970,* DHEW Pub. No. (HRA) 74-3105, 1973.

6
Demand, Supply, and Information in Health Care and Other Industries

Warren Greenberg

This chapter first examines demand and supply in the health care industry and compares them with demand and supply in other industries. Second, it examines how demand and supply have been manipulated by health care providers to realize greater returns in a way similar to patterns in other industries. Finally, it illustrates how altering the supply of a single commodity, information, can affect the quality and cost of health care.

Demand and Supply in Health Care

Demand. Unlike demand in most industries, the demand for health care has two components. The first is the demand by individuals, analogous to the demand for other goods and services in the economy, such as food and clothing. Approximately one-third of health care services is purchased by individuals. Studies have shown that, at least in purchasing visits to physicians, patients behave much as they do in purchasing other commodities. That is, the lower the net price (price charged minus insurance coverage), the more visits take place.[1]

The second component of demand may stem from individuals but is paid for by Medicare, Medicaid, commercial insurers, and Blue Cross–Blue Shield. The existence of these third-party insurers shifts the overall demand curves to the right in addition to lowering the net price to the individual. This shift assumes that the insurer is not actively engaged in cost containment and simply reimburses the provider for services rendered. A more active insurer that questions a physician's use of tests and procedures may be able to curtail a rightward shift of the demand curve.

Until the early 1980s most insurers were relatively passive about containing costs. Therefore, the shift of demand caused by the presence of insurance has been blamed by most economists for the rapid increase in health care costs. It is still unclear what effect the administration's prospective reimbursement initiatives for Medicare will have on the shape and movement of the demand curve. Since the government no longer reimburses at cost for Medicare enrollees, the demand curve is expected to shift to the left of where it would have been under cost reimbursement.

Supply. The supply of health services providers includes not only physicians but also alternative medical groups such as nurse midwives and psychologists. The supply of physicians is increasing dramatically. The ratio of physicians to the population will reach 245 per 100,000 by 1990, an increase from 148 per 100,000 in 1960.[2] The supply of medical professionals might be expanded even more rapidly, however, if alternative medical groups such as nurse midwives and psychologists were to gain staff privileges in hospitals.[3]

Another element of supply is the supply of health care institutions. The dominant health care institution is, of course, the acute care hospital, where 40 percent of all health care dollars are spent, but its dominance, like that of physicians, may be eroding. The fastest-growing institutions providing health care are nursing homes, and hospices have recently been authorized to receive reimbursement from Medicare.[4]

The dominance of institutions and services in health care is not unlike the behavior of firms in other industries. In the computer industry, for example, IBM has a dominant market share, but it must compete with hundreds of smaller computer manufacturers. In professional manpower markets economists with Ph.D.s must compete with those who have master's degrees.

An important aspect of supply in the health care sector is the supply of information, which has been a neglected area of study. I comment extensively on this aspect later in this chapter.

Simultaneous Relation of Demand and Supply

The relation between demand and supply in the determination of price is continuously evolving and simultaneous—in the health industry as in other industries. In the petroleum industry, for example, a restriction of supply by the OPEC nations increased the price of petroleum to monopolistic levels. In the short run a lesser quantity of gasoline was purchased. At the same time the higher price stimulated entry of new firms into the industry and technological advance. In the longer run demand was also affected since more automobiles with greater gas mileage were purchased. All these factors were responsible for the eventual decline in gasoline prices.

The supply of physicians' services has increased in response to high prices caused by a restriction of supply. For many of the first sixty years of the twentieth century, the American Medical Association was able to restrict the supply of physicians. The restricted supply raised fees for physicians' services and thus their incomes. But since 1960 the supply of physicians has increased. This increase has, I believe, made it easier for the payer (in many cases the insurer) to negotiate with physicians' groups. Preferred provider organizations, for example, which include physicians who generally accept lesser fees than physicians who do not belong to such groups, have been used by commercial insurers.[5]

Furthermore, because of rising costs, the number of health maintenance organizations (HMOs) entering the marketplace has substantially increased.[6] The availability of physicians no doubt made entry easier. Because of the entry of these alternative delivery systems, health services for those who are enrolled can be secured at lower prices. Even hospitals that need the services of house staff specialists are in a better bargaining position to employ them for lesser salaries. These trends might be surprising to those who have suggested that, in contrast to the traditional workings of supply and demand, a greater number of physicians means an increase in physicians' fees.[7]

Manipulation of Supply and Demand by Industry Groups

Very often firms within industries have chosen to restrict supply so as to receive larger market shares and higher profits. Often they have found that collaboration with the government has been the least costly method of restricting supply.

The airline industry, for example, and the Civil Aeronautics Board (CAB) set prices and restricted entry from the founding of the CAB in 1938 until the late 1970s.[8] Banks have imposed restrictions on entry into new geographic markets.[9] By restricting supply, the airline industry achieved higher prices and the banking industry higher profits than they would have achieved with increased competition.

Both the airline and banking industries are examples of government acquiescence and support of restriction of supply. Less frequent, but nevertheless not uncommon, are industry restrictions of supply without government support. One example is the widely cited *American Tobacco* case of 1946, in which the three largest cigarette firms—American Tobacco, Reynolds, and Liggett and Myers—ap-

peared to have restricted entry by predatory pricing.[10] The Supreme
Court supported the government's contention that this practice vio-
lated antitrust laws.[11]

Health care institutions have attempted to limit competition
through certificate-of-need laws enacted by state and federal governments. These laws were originally intended to limit construction of
health care facilities but have been used by providers to discourage
competition.[12] Health care groups have also attempted to limit competition without resort to legislation. HMOs trying to enter the marketplace have sometimes been thwarted by physicians' groups fearful of
alternative delivery systems.[13]

Supply of and Demand for Information in the Marketplace

Information is a service that producers are willing to supply and consumers are willing to demand. Information is demanded and supplied when stocks and bonds, life insurance, or real estate is purchased. The price we pay for these goods and services includes a price
for information from stockbrokers, insurance salespeople, and real
estate agents. Information is purchased directly when legal or medical
services are sought. In this section I examine information that may be
disseminated by the health service professions and by health care
institutions.

Supply of Information by Health Service Professions. Advertising by
the professions was prohibited by the American Medical Association
until 1982, when a Federal Trade Commission complaint alleging that
such prohibition was a restraint of trade was upheld by the Supreme
Court.[14] The American Dental Association, which had prohibited advertising by dentists, agreed to abide by the decision. The AMA had
been able to enforce its prohibition through sanctions that included
denial of staff privileges at hospitals and of medical society membership.[15]

Just as an increased supply of physicians may reduce physician
fees, an increased supply of information about physicians' services
may also reduce fees. Increased information may make it easier for
lower-priced sellers to be known, and it will reduce search costs for
potential buyers of services. For those physicians having relatively
lower prices, increased expenditures for their services may create
economies of scale of practice. Studies have found that, mostly because of economies of scale, prices of eyeglasses and prices charged
by optometrists were lower in states in which advertising was allowed.[16]

The supply of information might be helpful to individuals in choosing physicians (individuals pay 40 percent of physicians' charges) and at least reduce the costs of comparing fees and quality. Since physicians have thus far been reluctant to advertise overtly, we do not yet know the effects of the removal of the ban on advertising. (Physicians have not been hesitant, however, about indirect advertising. The Greater Laurel Beltsville Hospital in Laurel, Maryland for example, inserts a picture of physicians on their staff in a brochure distributed to all new residents of Prince George's County).

Evidence from other industries shows that increased advertising can lower prices by making demand curves more elastic.[17] Some economists still claim, however, that increased advertising can lead to higher prices by making demand curves more inelastic.[18]

Supply of Information by Health Service Institutions. There appears to be no overt collusion among hospitals to refrain from advertising. Rather, the American Hospital Association (AHA) has recommended strict guidelines, which appear to discourage aggressive marketing. The AHA's guidelines state that "self-aggrandizement of one hospital at the expense of another may be counterproductive, and, if inaccurate, could lead to charges of libel and claims for damages."[19] The guidelines suggest that *"quality comparisons, either direct or by implication, between one hospital's services, facilities, or employees and those of another hospital may be counterproductive, libelous, or difficult to present in a firm and objective manner."*[20] Hospitals have nevertheless begun to advertise, but superficially. Most advertising has been of amenities offered, quality of food, and convenience of location.[21]

An example drawn from cardiac surgery illustrates how the dissemination of information might lower costs and improve quality in the hospital sector. Recent studies showed that 55 percent of hospitals that perform open-heart surgery were performing fewer than 200 surgeries per year—the minimum for satisfactory results suggested by the U.S. Department of Health and Human Services for hospitals that have offered the service at least three years. Furthermore, recent research has found an apparent negative relation between the number of cardiac surgeries and mortality rates.[23] Research has also found that hospitals that perform a greater number of cardiac surgeries have lower average costs because of economies of scale.[24] Yet individuals continue to have surgery at low-volume hospitals.

American Hospital Association data for 1981 show the number of adult open-heart surgeries for hospitals in the five largest U.S. cities (hospitals that did no open-heart surgery do not figure in the means).[25]

New York City Hospitals	Number of Adult Open-Heart Surgeries
1. St. Luke's–Roosevelt Hospital Center	1,337
2. New York University Medical Center	981
3. Presbyterian Hospital in New York	725
4. Mount Sinai Hospital	531
5. St. Vincent's Hospital/Medical Center	498
6. Society of the New York Hospital	490
7. State University Hospital	375
8. Long Island Jewish–Hillside Medical Center	276
9. Lenox Hill Hospital	195
10. Veterans Administration Medical Center, New York City	125
11. Maimonides Medical Center	117
12. Bellevue Hospital Center	76
13. Veterans Administration Medical Center, Brooklyn	75
Mean number of surgeries	446

Chicago Hospitals	Number of Adult Open-Heart Surgeries
1. Rush–Presbyterian–St. Luke's Medical Center	926
2. Northwestern Memorial Hospital	512
3. Michael Reese Hospital Medical Center	300
4. Illinois Masonic Medical Center	278
5. University of Illinois Hospital	261
6. St. Joseph Hospital	179
7. Mercy Hospital Medical Center	160
8. Edgewater Hospital	138
9. Veterans Administration West Side Medical Center	128
10. Columbus Hospital	101
11. Grant Hospital of Chicago	78

12.	Mount Sinai Hospital Medical Center	78
13.	St. Mary of Nazareth Hospital Center	74
14.	Children's Memorial Hospital	6
	Mean number of surgeries	230

	Los Angeles Hospitals	*Number of Adult Open-Heart Surgeries*
1.	St. Vincent Medical Center	1,071
2.	Cedars-Sinai Medical Center	588
3.	Kaiser Foundation Hospital	328
4.	Hospital of The Good Samaritan	291
5.	Veterans Administration Wadsworth Medical Center	184
6.	University of California at Los Angeles Hospital	121
7.	Los Angeles County–University of Southern California Medical Center	85
8.	White Memorial Medical Center	81
9.	Martin Luther King, Jr., General Hospital	50
10.	Hollywood Presbyterian Medical Center	35
	Mean number of surgeries	283

	Philadelphia Hospitals	*Number of Adult Open-Heart Surgeries*
1.	Hahnemann Medical College and Hospital	865
2.	Lankenau Hospital	755
3.	Hospital of the University of Pennsylvania	703
4.	Thomas Jefferson University Hospital	700
5.	Graduate Hospital	434
6.	Hospital of the Medical College of Pennsylvania	299

7.	Presbyterian–University of Pennsylvania Medical Center	266
8.	Albert Einstein Medical Center	225
9.	Temple University Hospital	211
10.	Episcopal Hospital	66
	Mean number of surgeries	452

Detroit Hospitals	*Number of Adult* *Open-Heart Surgeries*
1. Harper Hospital	674
2. Henry Ford Hospital	410
3. St. John Hospital	325
4. Sinai Hospital of Detroit	273
5. Detroit Receiving Hospital	2
Mean number of surgeries	337

The wide dispersion of the number of cardiac surgeries within each of the five cities is of interest. In New York City, for example, although St. Luke's–Roosevelt Hospital Center performed 1,337 cardiac operations, 588 individuals went to hospitals that performed fewer than 200 operations. This pattern is repeated throughout the United States.

Given that the price of hospital care to the patient is essentially the same for any hospital in which surgery is performed (the third-party insurer pays an average of more than 90 percent of hospital expenditures regardless of the choice of hospital), why would individuals elect to have major surgery at low-volume hospitals?

It is important to emphasize that the number of cardiac operations per hospital is used in this analysis as a proxy for the degree of risk associated with the surgery. Specifically, the working hypothesis here is that the greater number of procedures of this type conducted at a hospital, the lower the risk. Research evidence supports such a relationship, and some observers have explained it by the greater ability to anticipate complications and the increased experience of surgical teams at hospitals performing a large number of procedures.

Other factors, however, clearly affect the extent of risk associated with a particular operation. The skill and experience of the surgeon conducting that one operation, for example, will also be important in the determination of the outcome of the surgery.

Other factors that may influence the choice of hospital include the geographic convenience of the hospital, the degree of emergency of the surgery, and the religious affiliation of the hospital. The hospital selected may also be influenced by previous hospitalizations and the recommendations of internists or cardiologists.

With these caveats in mind, it is useful to observe from the dispersion of cardiac surgeries among hospitals in an area that surgeries are not all clustered in one or two high-volume hospitals that specialize in open-heart surgery. This suggests either that some of the other factors just noted outweigh the relation between volume and risk (assuming that it holds) or that patients and their physicians do not have or are not acting on information about these volume differences.

My current research seeks to determine the relative weights that individuals put on information and other factors in decisions to have cardiac surgery at particular hospitals. Furthermore, it examines the types of information available from consulting physicians and cardiologists. We need further research to isolate the importance of information in the process of choosing a hospital for a medical procedure.

The Importance of the Study of Information in the Hospital Market. I have suggested that the existence of many low-volume hospitals that perform cardiac surgery may, in fact, reflect a failure of information supplied in the hospital marketplace. Suppose, however, that an increased amount of information, such as the number of cardiac surgeries by hospital, and the caveats to be used in interpreting it were supplied to the patient. Hospitals that performed fewer than the optimal number of procedures might lose patients and might eventually have to eliminate their cardiac surgery units. Hospitals that performed a satisfactory number of procedures might expand. The result could be higher overall quality and lower costs. An increased supply of information might, therefore, help allocate the delivery of health care services more efficiently than certificate-of-need and other health planning laws.

Summary and Conclusions

This chapter has shown how the basic principles of supply and demand work in the health care marketplace and how similar their workings are to the interplay of supply and demand for most other goods and services in the economy. It has also suggested that the normal flow of supply and demand is often inhibited by special interest groups that would benefit from restriction of supply or expansion of demand.

The supply of information is a special focus of this chapter. I have suggested that an increased supply of information in the hospital marketplace might have profound effects on the quality and cost of health care. Additional research on the magnitude of the effects is warranted.

Without information about the cost, quality, and safety of health services, consumers may select providers solely on the basis of a convenient location or the suggestion of other providers. With information, consumers can opt for doctors and hospitals that they believe are most likely to provide them with a successful health outcome. Even with a great supply of information, physicians' attachment to hospitals may create barriers to a perfectly rational distribution of health care resources. But the greater and more useful the information, the better will be the match between patients' problems and providers' capacity for solving them.

Notes

1. Joseph P. Newhouse et al., "Some Interim Results from a Controlled Trial of Cost Sharing in Health Insurance," *New England Journal of Medicine*, vol. 305 (December 1981), pp. 1501-7.

2. U.S. Congress, Office of Technology Assessment, *Forecast of Physician Supply and Requirements* (Washington, D.C., April 1980), p. 22.

3. See, for example, "Midwives Seek Delivery from Discrimination," *New York Times*, August 7, 1983.

4. "Medicare Rate Set for Hospice Care of Terminally Ill," *New York Times*, August 18, 1983.

5. "Insurance Plan Considered Here Angers Doctors," *Washington Post*, August 23, 1983.

6. Health Insurance Association of America, *Source Book of Health Insurance, 1982-83* (Washington, D.C.), p. 8.

7. See Robert G. Evans, "Supplier-Induced Demand: Some Empirical Evidence and Implications," in Mark Perlman, ed., *The Economics of Health and Medical Care* (London: Macmillan, 1974), pp. 162-73, for a contrary view.

8. Lawrence J. White, *Reforming Regulation* (Englewood Cliffs, N.J.: Prentice Hall, 1981), p. 32.

9. William G. Shepherd and Clair Wilcox, *Public Policies toward Business* (Homewood, Ill.: Richard D. Irwin, 1979), p. 488.

10. American Tobacco Co. et al. v. U.S., 328 U.S. 781 (1946).

11. Ibid.

12. Clark C. Havighurst, *Deregulating the Health Care Industry* (Cambridge, Mass.: Ballinger, 1982).

13. See the earlier attempts of the American Medical Association to stymie the growth of the Group Health Association in the late 1930s in American Medical Association v. United States, 317 U.S. 519 (1943). There have been additional incidents since this case. See Paul Starr, *The Social Transformation of*

American Medicine (New York: Basic Books, 1982), pp. 298–306.

14. American Medical Association v. FTC, 452 U.S. 960 (1982).

15. See Reuben Kessel, "Price Discrimination in Medicine," *Journal of Law and Economics* (October 1958), pp. 20–53.

16. See Lee Benham, "The Effects of Advertising on the Price of Eyeglasses," *Journal of Law and Economics* (October 1972), pp. 337–52; see also James Begun and Roger Feldman, "A Social and Economic Analysis of Professional Regulation in Optometry," *NCHSR Research Report Series* (April 1981), PHS 81-235.

17. See James M. Ferguson, *Advertising and Competition: Theory, Measurement, and Fact* (Cambridge, Mass.: Ballinger, 1974); and Keith B. Leffler, "Persuasion or Information? The Economics of Prescription Drug Advertising," *Journal of Law and Economics*, vol. 24 (April 1981), pp. 45–74.

18. See William J. Comanor and Thomas A. Wilson, *Advertising and Market Power* (Cambridge, Mass.: Harvard University Press, 1974).

19. See American Hospital Association, "Guidelines—Advertising by Hospitals" (Chicago, 1977), p. 2.

20. Ibid. (italics added).

21. Richard E. McDonald, "The Health Care Industry Discovers Broadcasting," *Broadcasting*, September 20, 1982, p. 18.

22. Robert H. Kennedy et al., "Cardiac-Catheterization and Cardiac-Surgical Facilities," *New England Journal of Medicine*, vol. 307 (October 1982), pp. 986–93.

23. Harold S. Luft et al., "Should Operations Be Regionalized?" *New England Journal of Medicine* (December 1979), pp. 1364–69.

24. Steven A. Finkler, "Cost-Effectiveness of Regionalization: The Heart Surgery Example," *Inquiry* (Fall 1979), pp. 264–70.

25. American Hospital Association, Hospital Data Center, *1981 Annual Survey, Hospitals with Open-Heart and Cardiac Catheterization Facilities*, unpaged and undated.

7

Supply Responses to Market and Regulatory Forces in Health Care

Richard J. Arnould and Charles B. Van Vorst

The literature on health care costs focuses heavily on two alleged problems—an excessive amount of services consumed and an inefficient system of delivering whatever quantity of services is purchased. These twin problems stem, in part, from the unique characteristics of health care delivery that make the markets difficult to regulate and from the highly emotional and personal effects of health care on individuals. Attempts to regulate these problems away have in some instances failed to achieve any results and in others exacerbated the problem of rapidly rising health care costs by generating perverse demand and supply incentives.

Recent attention has focused on the use of market mechanisms to alleviate the rising cost of health care. These mechanisms include methods of shifting a portion of the financial risk from third-party payers to providers and consumers. If this shifting is done properly, it should provide market incentives for efficient production and consumption of health care services by moderating demand and encouraging suppliers to compete for the limited health care dollars. Some alternative delivery and finance systems—such as health maintenance organizations (HMOs) and preferred provider organizations (PPOs)—provide a limited test of the market-oriented approach to cost containment.

Limiting growth in the dollars devoted to health care will generate supply responses as providers seek to develop more efficient means of production. In this chapter we focus on the supply responses to market-oriented reimbursement mechanisms. These responses will include organizational and financial changes, as well as changes in relations among providers. Hospitals will integrate into related services, relations between hospitals and physicians will change, and these changes will affect other providers. Finally, shrinking resources will force providers to seek new sources for their capital needs.

Before discussing the supply responses to market mechanisms, it is useful to review the response of health care providers to the incentives of the regulatory approach to reform. This discussion sets a conceptual framework of how reliance on market forces can be used to change incentives, which will lead to the supply-side responses discussed later. We conclude with a discussion of the adequacy of market forces in providing health care services to the poor and with some caveats about quality.

Regulation: Its Perverse Effect on Economic Efficiency

The government participates in health care markets in two ways: as a purchaser of care under Medicare and Medicaid and as a regulator. Mark Pauly has pointed out that the confusion of these roles has led to inefficient supply responses and rising demand.[1] It has been argued elsewhere that inefficiency has emerged because the industry is not conducive to traditional methods of regulation.[2] Traditional regulatory economics offers a conceptual framework for predicting and analyzing supply responses to either market-oriented incentives or government regulation.

Expansion of Supply. Federal entitlements and tax policies have stimulated the demand for health care. Specifically, Medicare and Medicaid were designed to increase access to health care among the elderly and low-income households, while the tax treatment of employers' contributions to employee health insurance stimulated the demand for more comprehensive private sector insurance coverage. In turn, government subsidies have expanded the size and number of hospitals and the number of medical professionals to meet this increasing demand. Historically, government policy emphasized promoting both the accessibility and the quality of care.

In response to the increased demand for care from physicians and hospitals, the need for health manpower and health facilities increased. The government responded to this demand (which it had stimulated in the first place) by implementing supply-side subsidies to institutional and educational markets.

Direct subsidies provided funding for new hospital construction and renovation of existing health care facilities under the Hill-Burton program, initiated in 1946. Medical services were also provided through Veterans Administration, state, and local government hospitals. In addition to these direct subsidies, more indirect subsidies included the granting of tax-exempt status to nonprofit hospitals and Blue Cross plans as well as state assistance in financing hospital bond issues.[3]

To help ensure an adequate supply of health professionals, government support was provided to expand existing programs and create new education programs for physicians, nurses, and allied health professionals. Between 1964 and 1978, $1 billion in federal funds was provided to support nursing education. The number of registered nurses graduating increased 7.5 percent annually between 1966 and 1973.[4] Allied health professionals gained attention and support in the early 1970s in response to the shortages of primary care in rural areas. Various forms of legislation were passed between 1971 and 1977 to support the growth of this group of providers, including the authorization of Medicare and Medicaid reimbursement for services delivered by "physician-extenders" in rural, medically underserved areas.[5]

Major increases in federal programs to expand medical education began in 1963 and continued through the 1970s. The predominant forms of support were loans and grants for teaching and research facilities and funding for student loan programs. These brought about an increase in the number of medical schools from 86 in 1960 to 125 in 1979 and of graduates from 7,081 in 1960 to 14,966 in 1979.

In an efficient market system, as demand for a good or service rises, the price will also rise until the higher price serves to ration the available supply. Increases in supply will offset or retard the price increases and thus expand output without increasing unit prices. Available evidence indicates, however, that increases in the supply of health care have *increased*, not decreased, both unit prices and units of output. This supply response is predictable because of the following market conditions: Producers have few incentives to compete for health care dollars because those dollars are simply expanded when more services are provided. Consumers have few incentives to question medical authorities about the number of services provided or the configuration of treatment patterns because their marginal cost of services is close to zero. Therefore, expansion of supply, normally a cost-retarding factor, may have had little, if any, favorable effect on the cost of medical services.

Control of Supply. The inability to control increases in costs associated with increases in demand through the expansion of supply led to what Zeckhauser and Zook have labeled regulation by "command and control"; that is, the government commands that health care be supplied and attempts to control efficiency by regulating specific inputs used to supply health care services.[7] None of these policies, however, has been designed to provide incentives for efficient determination of demand by consumers or efficient determination of supply by producers.

Professional standards review organizations (PSROs) were instituted to eliminate services that deviate from an accepted norm, that is, services where the social benefits fall short of the social costs. Obviously, this will be effective only in situations where the benefits and costs can be adequately documented and where incentives exist for most suppliers to operate at the efficient norms. In many areas of health care, however, the relation between inputs and outcomes has not been well documented and may be difficult to document accurately if past incentives have led to inefficient supply responses as a norm.[8]

The second method used to control supply costs was to require review of hospital investments in capital assets over certain minimum limits. In health care markets, this has taken the form of certificate-of-need (CON) requirements. A well-known tenet of regulatory economics is that efforts to control investment in one input, such as a specific type of capital, when incentives are not provided to minimize total costs, are likely not only to fail but to lead to other costly distortions in the production process.

Watts and Updegraff found no evidence that CON requirements reduced capital expenditures in New York.[9] Bicknell and Walsh found that they reduced the growth of licensed acute care beds in Massachusetts, but over the same period increased the rate of growth of beds devoted to psychiatric, extended, and special care.[10] Sloan and Steinwald argue that CON regulation will restrict the entry of any new, potentially more efficient providers and protect the existing configurations of suppliers by protecting the suppliers from new competitors.[11] To the degree that the status quo is inefficient, this inefficiency is solidified through regulation.

Finally, Salkever and Bice found that while CON regulation has reduced the rate of growth in hospital beds, it has been unable effectively to address the substantial increase in employees per bed and auxiliary services per bed and has therefore been generally ineffective as a method of controlling the total costs of health care.[12]

A lesson can be learned from attempts to regulate price and output (through entry control) of airline services.[13] Inhibited from competing on the basis of price and protected from competition from new entrants into their markets, the existing carriers turned to expensive forms of quality competition. Substantial excess capacity resulted from the larger number of flights between cities accompanied by the use of larger and less efficient aircraft. Firms were operating below the efficient production function. Aggregate benefits to airlines were not great because economic rents accruing as a result of entry controls were competed away in the cost of providing these elements of quality.

The health care sector has performed similarly. As stated earlier, entry control (CON) has resulted in excess capacity and promoted various forms of quality in health care markets. The average occupancy rate in U.S. community hospitals was only 73.6 percent in 1979, down from 77.3 percent in 1970.[14] Many coronary intensive care units operate below the recommended capacities necessary for quality control, and expensive equipment for other forms of treatment is severely underused by some institutions. These distortions arise from attempts to set "competitive" prices through regulation. Errors in the estimates of competitive prices, which the complexity of the product makes likely, cause supply responses that generate inefficiencies in the markets being regulated.

The government and the private sector have also attempted to limit health care costs by placing limits on covered costs for certain services. These limits have been incomplete and have not covered all services. Until 1982, for example, various cost caps and the Medicare section 223 limits on total reimbursement related only to daily service charges (such as hospital room and board). Limiting the government payment for routine daily service but not for high-technology ancillary services shifted costs to services not covered by the limits, which were included in the controlled category in 1982. In addition, placing limits on certain payers and not on others has distorted treatment patterns and has had little effect on total health care costs.

To this point, we have argued that efforts to control health care costs by controlling certain elements of supply have been systematically unsuccessful and in some instances may have exacerbated the problem, in large part because of certain characteristics inherent in the health care industry. While insurance exists to protect against financial risk, the complexity of the services makes it difficult to define the limits of insurance coverage; so significant "moral hazard" emerges. Tax policies, reimbursement methods, and subsidizing the expansion of providers have offered few incentives to control demand or to supply services efficiently.

A Changing Climate in the Public and Private Sectors

Remarkably, a desire to control health expenditures is emerging in the 1980s despite reluctance to change regulatory policies that provide

111

perverse cost control incentives. The difficulties of many American industries competing in world markets have led to close scrutiny of all costs, which has often disclosed that employee health insurance is one of the fastest-growing employee benefits. In 1983 total public and private expenditures for health care in the United States accounted for over 40 percent of total employee benefit expenditures. Even though tax policies disguise the true cost to the private sector, the sheer magnitude of expenditures has caused employers great concern.

Demographic changes provide additional reason for concern about public sector expenditures for health care. The population of the United States is aging. In 1950 some 92 percent of the population was under sixty-five. In 1980 only 89 percent was under sixty-five, and by 2000 less than 80 percent will be under sixty-five.[15] This aging of the population has two significant effects on revenue requirements to cover government outlays for health care, particularly Medicare payments. The obvious effect is that a smaller portion of the working population is burdened with payment of health care bills for a growing population covered by Medicare. Even more significant, demands for health care services increase substantially with age. Therefore, it has been predicted that the Medicare fund will be bankrupt in the next decade unless more efficient methods are found to provide these services, coverage is reduced, or taxes are increased.

Market forces are present on the supply side to produce intense competition for the health care dollar. Hill-Burton funds and public support of the expansion of medical education have created excess supply. As in the air transport industry, when regulation thwarted the penalties for excess supply, there were only limited incentives to compete for business. Limiting increases in expenditures for health care will change these incentives. Hospitals that are able to maintain or even increase occupancy will make it difficult for others to generate returns adequate to maintain or improve existing facilities with new cost-efficient technologies. Similarly, doctors will have to provide services efficiently and compete, in a market sense, to fill their schedules.

Likely responses to these competitive pressures by the medical profession are predictable since it is widely perceived that the profession is driven by the profit motive. But the preponderance in the hospital sector of not-for-profit institutions with less well defined economic objectives makes the prediction of responses more tenuous.[16] Two factors will spur nonprofit hospitals to compete. The first is the general shortage of funds for capital. The interest rates required to sell tax-exempt bonds for health facilities have placed considerable strain on not-for-profit hospitals' revenue requirements. The second factor is the growth in the market significance of proprietary hospitals, whose goals are clearly to maximize profits, places further pressures on the not-for-profit hospitals to increase their efficiency.

Past policies have permitted inefficient pricing structures that have distorted efficient resource configurations. There has been little incentive to substitute ambulatory care for inpatient care, for example, or to employ an efficient mixture of licensed physicians and allied health professionals. If entry barriers are reduced, not only are more efficiently configured providers likely to enter health care markets, but specialized vendors are likely to "cream-skim."

In summary, there is substantial theoretical evidence that the elimination of many costly forms of regulation and the reliance on prospectively determined market prices will greatly increase efficiency in health care markets. Financial, political, and demographic forces are lining up to enforce the market mechanism. One precaution about market-determined outcomes must be emphasized, however. Governmental units purchasing services for Medicare and Medicaid patients have substantial monopsony power in many health services markets. Using that power to drive prices below their competitive levels will reduce the quality of care, by driving recipients of publicly reimbursed services either into longer queues or to lower-quality providers. Therefore, as states adopt market pricing mechanisms such as competitive bidding or voucher systems, quality standards that can be monitored must be a part of the contractual arrangement unless a tiered medical system is desired. If controlled effectively, competition will bring about numerous supply responses as providers attempt to find organizational and input configurations that permit more efficient delivery of health care. Some of these responses are discussed in the next section of this chapter.

Supply-Side Changes

The forces outlined are bringing about structural and organizational changes by the suppliers of health care. At the heart of these changes is the interaction of shrinking financial resources available for health care with an ever-increasing demand for health care services. This has brought about the seeming paradox of payers and direct consumers demanding the same or greater amounts of service for less money. Thus the burden on the supply side of the market is to provide services more efficiently.

The current oversupply of hospital beds and the projected oversupply of physicians have added impetus to organizational, structural, and financial changes by providers. Conventional views of health care—how it is delivered and how it should be financed—are changing.

These changes have effects beyond the hospital and the physician, as we currently conceive of their roles. They are affecting the traditional relations between physicians and hospitals and have begun to affect other providers of health care. Home care services, extended care, respite care, geriatric day care, transportation, supply and material services, and insurance all have been and will be changing.

The expenditures for each major subpart of the health care system for 1960 and 1980 are shown in table 7-1. Each part has its own characteristics and role in the delivery of health care. Clearly, the greatest expenditures for health care have been for hospitals and physicians.

Each subsystem has traditionally performed its functions cooperatively with other subsystems, but not in a truly coordinated or integrated way. Perhaps the greatest degree of coordination has been between the physician and the hospital in delivering inpatient care. Even this integration has been limited, however, and not based on truly common objectives.

The predominant lack of integration of the subsystems of health care delivery is a result of such historical forces as reimbursement practices, licensure, regulation, and professional prerogatives. These historical policy-shaping forces are products of the lack of a longitudinally consistent central direction-setting mechanism for health care delivery.

The traditional roles and functions of most of the subparts become "codified" and relatively fixed in their abilities to change traditional behavior significantly. Changes brought about over the past several years by cost containment programs relate principally to hospitals and more recently to physicians.

The following discussion analyzes providers' responses to the changing nature of regulation and reimbursement from the perspectives of three major groups: acute care inpatient institutions (hospitals), physicians, and other providers and major services. Its intent is illustrative since the variety of relations among subcomponents of each group makes absolute definition difficult. Moreover, many of these changes have just begun to occur. Therefore, final results are only predictive.

Acute Inpatient Care Institutions (Hospitals). The greatest change has been occurring within the acute care and specialty hospitals. These institutions, because of their share of total expenditures and

114

TABLE 7-1
NATIONAL HEALTH EXPENDITURES, BY MAJOR TRADITIONAL HEALTH
CARE PROVIDERS, 1960 AND 1980
(percent)

	1960	1980
Inpatient acute care institutions	33.8	40.3
Physicians' services	21.1	18.9
Long-term-care institutions	2.0	8.4
Other providers, including dental, home care, chiropractors	14.1	10.8
Pharmaceutical services	13.6	7.8
Supply and material services	2.9	2.1
Insurance and third-party brokerage services	4.1	4.2
Other	8.4	7.5
Total percent	100.0	100.0
Total expenditures ($ billions)	26.9	247.2

SOURCE: R.M. Gibson and D.R. Waldo, "National Health Expenditures, 1980," *Health Care Financing Review*, HCFA Pub. No. 03123, Health Care Financing Administration, Washington, D.C., 1981.

their relatively small number, have traditionally been the direct target of government cost containment regulations and initiatives. They have felt the most direct effects of cost-based reimbursement deficits and the complex problems of how to maintain their profitability and long-range viability.

Strategic planning and marketing. Current forces for change are requiring (and in some cases allowing) hospitals to review their mission and purpose critically in an attempt to rationalize long-range planning. What services and programs are needed within the context of their financial reimbursement outlook is a critical question for each of these institutions. No longer can providers rely on retrospective cost reimbursement to fill in the gaps of financial requirements. No longer can every institution be all things to all people. New appreciation for marketing and management of the demand of health care services is providing increased focus on the wants and demands of the individual consumer, advertising and promotion, services offered in a manner that creates consumer satisfaction and acceptance, more attractive facilities and amenities related to but not necessarily essential to care, and increased concern for the consumers' needs for timely and convenient services. This more external view of the role of the institution is not uniform throughout the nation's hospitals, but it is spreading and causing boards of trustees, management, physicians, and informed members of the community to reevaluate not only the hospital's purpose but its ability to survive in its present form.

Specific examples are drawn from the authors' relationship with the Carle Foundation and the Carle Clinic Association in Urbana, Illinois, as well as from other sources. The Carle Foundation is a not-for-profit provider of a broad range of health services, principally the ownership and management of the 283-bed Carle Foundation Hospital. The Carle Clinic Association, which leases space from the Carle Foundation, is a for-profit, 165-member multispecialty group practice including most medical and surgical subspecialties.

Changing market forces have necessitated many changes in strategic planning and the adoption of a more market-oriented view of the role of hospitals in the communities they serve. Improvement and expansion of data bases linking clinical, demographic, and cost information are essential. They will provide better knowledge of clients and the financial and competitive effects on the hospital of alternative methods used in their care. In the Carle Foundation, a doubling of the marketing and promotions staff, including the employment of an executive with broad marketing experience, has been necessary to lead the activity.

Market analysis in the Carle setting has resulted in the provision of services that focus on the clients' needs. These services range from a program to redefine for staff the concept of the patient and his friends or relatives as guests to expanded amenities, including valet parking, doorman service, a patient complaint hotline, and specialized patient appointment nurse services to counsel and direct patients to the medically and economically appropriate specialists in the organization. Each of these changes relates to efforts to compete efficiently for the shrinking dollars that result from reduced demand for inpatient services.

Multihospital Systems. As health care delivery has become more complex, it has become more capital and managerial intensive. Inefficiencies that result from poor management are less likely to be hidden as we move away from retrospective cost-based reimbursement systems. A prevalent method for acquiring management resources is the formation of multihospital systems. This has occurred through various forms of altered control arrangements from mergers, acquisitions, affiliations, and contract management. The point on the continuum chosen by a particular hospital depends on a number of variables. The goal is to achieve institutional stability through multi-institutional linkages that offer the advantages of increased access to capital, increased commitment to planning, increased potential for collaboration and information sharing, increased market power through larger size, increased expertise resulting from a broader base for recruitment, and increased innovation for problem solving.

The greatest growth in multihospitals has been among for-profit companies. For-profit hospitals have grown from 53,000 beds, or 6 percent of total hospital facilities, in 1970 to 88,000 beds, or 9 percent of the total, in 1981.[17] This growth occurred not only in ownership and lease arrangements but also in contract-managed facilities. By 1980, 585 hospitals were being managed under contract by outside organizations.

The hospitals using contract management range in size from 35 to over 500 beds and operate in the public and the private sectors. Both nonprofit and for-profit hospitals are being successfully managed by contract services. Of particular interest is the successful use of contract management in publicly owned hospitals and in hospitals operated under religious auspices. In both cases outside managers seem able to make the "tough decisions" that managers who relate strongly to their constituencies cannot.

Growth of not-for-profit multiorganizational arrangements is a more recent phenomenon and one that should continue as hospitals and their constituent communities evaluate their ability to provide their future managerial and capital needs independently. Figure 7–1 shows the range of relationships for consideration, each with its own set of advantages and disadvantages.

The Carle Foundation Hospital is just concluding its first three-year contract for the management of a thirty-bed hospital within twenty-five miles of its main campus. A second three-year contract has just begun. It is clear from the experience of this management relationship and from discussions with other institutions that market forces bringing about a shrinking demand for hospital services are causing many institutions to consider multihospital relationships along the continuum of possibilities so as to have access to management and capital to remain viable. Clearly, a major aspect of these changes in structure is the providers' incentive to find methods of operating more efficiently. The risks in the environment and the incentives for the major stakeholders to undergo structural change must increase before major relocations in the marketplace can occur.

Reorganization. Either independently, or as concomitants of greater strategic planning or of the development of multi-institutional links, major changes are occurring in the traditional corporate structure of a

FIGURE 7-1
Continuum of Multihospital System Relationships

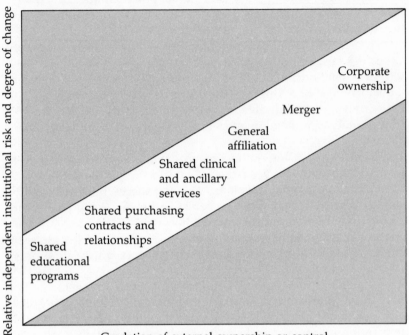

growing number of hospitals. The specific objectives of any institution's reevaluation of structure must rest on its individual objectives, but generally the objectives of current reorganization have been to

- achieve greater organizational flexibility for horizontal or vertical integration with other organizations or activities
- remove regulatory jurisdiction, such as certificate-of-need for services, or functions to compete on an equal footing with other subsystems whose actions are less restricted by health planning laws
- avoid delays, expense, and strategic disclosure of information associated with health regulation
- move profitable services out of the heavily regulated, cost-based hospital environment, thereby maximizing overall profitability
- provide other organizational vehicles for diversification and additional sources of revenue
- provide management flexibility on a separate operational basis but with the ability to aggregate assets and revenues for greater financial leverage and borrowing capacity.

118

The traditional corporate structure under which most hospitals were organized brought into one legal entity the assets, revenues, management, and license of an institution. Demographics, regulatory changes, and the technological nature of health care delivery have created problems for this form of legal entity, including potentially serious conflicts between strategies for maximizing reimbursement, financing capital, meeting CON requirements, and achieving organizational efficiency.

Figure 7–2 shows the corporate structure of the Carle Foundation, which moved from a single legal entity to one in which the hospital became a separate and distinct provider. The foundation has become a "parent," which holds major assets and supplies managerial services under contract for the hospital, other Carle corporations, and other institutions. External fund raising is focused in the Carle Development Foundation. Non-hospital-based services are located in Carle Health Care Incorporated. This unit's principal activity is the development of a home care program and a medical film distribution division. Carle Management Services Corporation is a for-profit entity, which provides full managerial and health care services. This institutional form permits depreciable assets to be placed in an entity where ownership can be used effectively to offset taxable income.

Regardless of the reasons for an individual institution's reorganization strategy, the long-term benefit lies in a change in its attitude and perceptions. The principal focus should shift to minimizing costs and integrating health care services in such a way as to produce efficiencies in production. The flexibility afforded by reorganization, if so used, will be a positive supply-side response rather than a short-range strategy that may increase health care costs.

It appears that truly innovative providers view the hospital as a factor of production rather than a static "place." But forcing prudent examination of how health care of high quality can best be delivered most efficiently, reorganization moves the institution's board and administration out of a narrow and self-centered view of the hospital to a more integrated view of health care.

Diversification. Hospitals have sought other forms of revenue in an attempt to maintain their viability. Such a strategy addresses the present shortfall in Medicare and Medicaid reimbursement in relation to full financial requirements. Hospitals' perceptions of their costs and hospital reimbursement through federal programs are billions of dollars apart. The shortfall, or subsidy, has been absorbed by institutions, shifted to other patients, or replaced by other nonoperating revenue.[18]

119

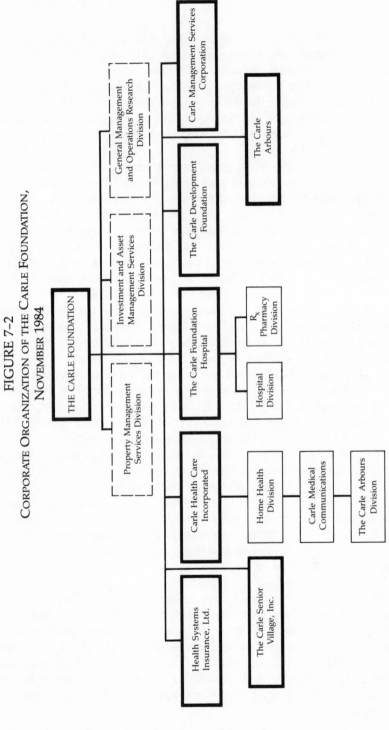

FIGURE 7-2
CORPORATE ORGANIZATION OF THE CARLE FOUNDATION, NOVEMBER 1984

SOURCE: The Carle Foundation.

120

As discussed throughout this chapter, our traditional regulatory and reimbursement systems give consumers and providers incentives to shift costs. Recent inflation and the economic downturn in the early 1980s, coupled with the supply-and-demand forces in the health care system, have brought this "hidden tax" into sharper focus.[19]

The problem will not be solved by diversification aimed at increasing non-hospital-related income to offset or cross-subsidize hospital-related losses. Institutions that undertake diversification with such a strategy will only forestall real problem solving.

Supply-side diversification should be occurring not only to expand revenue but to use the added functions and the income they generate to expand and integrate structures and thus to provide more efficient treatment patterns and more effective means to control the costs of those providing services. Carle Clinic's creation of a health maintenance organization (HMO) diversified it into a new insurance market. Its purpose was not that of a traditional insurer but was to expand its market share by offering a financing mechanism attractive to many consumers and to stimulate more efficient treatment patterns. The development of five ambulatory care offices (offsite and in other geographic locations) is a form of diversification into more local and therefore more accessible primary care and, like the HMO, reduces reliance on outside referrals.

The development of the Carle Home Care Agency, innovative relations with extended care institutions, and the establishment of a wellness center are further examples of "integrating" diversification. The provision of sports medicine injury and evaluation services to over 110 schools in the area is another example of a strategy designed to promote related business activity.

A 236-bed skilled nursing facility has been purchased for the provision of long-term care and as an efficient location for hospital patients needing less care than provided in the acute care hospital. In addition, a retail pharmacy with five off-campus locations serves the general community and provides for the pharmaceutical needs of the HMO enrollees. The foundation has also entered the durable medical equipment business as a retailer.

The Carle Foundation has traditionally served as landlord for all Carle entities and has built over 210,000 square feet of medical offices. These activities bring in non-cost-based reimbursement income and "integrate" the continued development of physician services. Other forms of diversification include the ownership of a gasoline station and of commercial and residential property and the beginning of a nationally focused company to distribute educational films.

121

Physicians' Services. Historically, the delivery of physicians' services has been individualized and decentralized in the United States. Of the 389,000 nonfederal physicians actively practicing, 88,000 practice in groups.[20] The majority of physicians are in solo practice or in limited association with other physicians. The demand for physicians' services grew so steadily after World War II as to obviate the perceived need for organized marketing and referral systems or for other kinds of practice structures aimed at improving the volume of patients served.

The recently projected oversupply of physicians has heightened physicians' concern with market share. Moreover, the actions of many hospitals over the past several years in "repositioning" themselves in relation to the growing trend toward outpatient care has been a source of concern and friction. Physicians' responses include greater emphasis on performing outpatient procedures and tests in their offices.

These moves by physicians to diversification—through expanding their normal "lines of business" or incurring overhead to allow the services to be performed internally rather than externally—are generated by attempts to control costs and to compete effectively in the market. Efforts to reduce costs by performing services outside the traditional hospital or individual practitioner's office have led to free-standing ambulatory surgical centers and free-standing emergency care centers operated either by independent physicians or by for-profit corporations. These units began major marketing efforts in specialized lines of care. They result from cost containment programs and changes in regulation that allow greater flexibility to physicians than to hospitals, a technological evolution that allows greater flexibility in treatment and resources, and an individual and corporate concern for market share and profit maximization.

As hospitals face increased use of outpatient services, shorter lengths of stay, and shrinking health care resources, a reorientation of their traditional role and their largely independent and nonintegrated medical staffs is occurring. Changes in conventional assumptions of how health care is rendered and financed are placing all providers at risk (though unevenly). Financial risk is further increased through recently enacted prospective reimbursement systems, which limit inpatient reimbursement to a predetermined amount based on the patient's diagnosis, not on the amount of resources used in providing the care. It is the physician, not the institution, who determines the type and amount of resources used. These more recent changes and the changes expected in methods of reimbursing physicians will establish a milieu of substantial change among those with major stakes in the health care system and will force careful reexamination of the relations between hospital administrators and medical staffs in the areas of utilization review and quality assurance.

Growth of Group Practice. The growth of group practice from 16.4 percent of professionally active physicians in 1970 to 22.7 percent in 1980 may reflect a recognition that the highly decentralized delivery of physicians' services poses a market risk that can be partially offset by cooperation and integration.[21] The advantages of closer collegial and economic relations include convenience, referral, and consultative benefits for the physician. Benefits to society may emerge through the ability of group practices to provide better medical care more efficiently. The greater efficiency of closed-panel HMOs provided by group practices than of other less associative models has been thoroughly documented in reduced hospital admission rates, reduced lengths of stay, and reduced production costs per treatment.[22]

From society's perspective, the objectives of hospitals and physicians will need to merge to respond to our nation's health care needs efficiently. From a provider's perspective, more integration and goal sharing will lead to cost-effective operations and long-term survival. The organization of physicians into group practices will increase to foster a greater integration of the objectives of suppliers of physicians' services and the scale of operations necessary to develop and market new delivery systems efficiently. Unique and innovative relations between physicians and hospitals are developing, which integrate their historical roles and contribute to increased efficiency, expanded market share, and role predictability.

Such a relationship exists between the Carle Clinic Association and the Carle Foundation Hospital. They trace their roots to a common beginning and share a main campus in Urbana, Illinois. They have more unity of objectives than is customary between suppliers in today's health care system because of their parallel development through a myriad of consultative, collaborative, and contractual relations.

Historically, the growth in beds at the Carle Foundation Hospital has been considerably below the growth of physicians' services, in part because the synergistic relationship between the two organizations has permitted innovative "merging" of hospital and physicians' services. The production efficiencies gained from this integration are evident in the recently published results of hospital use in Illinois.

In 1981 Champaign County, in which the Carle Foundation Hospital has 35 percent of the inpatient beds, attracted inpatients from other counties at the third highest rate in the state. The vast majority of the population residing in Champaign County remained in the county for their care. More important, the hospital use rate for Champaign County residents was the lowest in the state among counties with equal or smaller population bases.

Additional inferences can be drawn from hospital cost patterns developed in 1979 by the state of Illinois to categorize hospitals by intensity levels. The Carle Foundation Hospital was categorized as a high-intensity hospital whose case costs were below the statewide average for that category.

Finally, the cost of total services provided through the Carle organizations was competitive with the 1983 state of Illinois bids for HMO contracts for state employees. Carle's HMO, CarleCare, offered a price structure competitive with those of comparable benefit plans, which included HMOs in metropolitan Chicago and competing Champaign County HMOs. These examples show the production efficiencies that can be obtained through greater integration and shared objectives.

Broadened Delivery Prerogatives. The complexity of the insured services, the unique relations between insurers and providers, and the tax treatment afforded both insurers and the payers of health insurance have offered third parties very limited incentives to take an active role in moderating the costs of health services by exerting their potential influence over delivery practices.[23] The purchasing power of the services has thus been in the hands of a third party, with the prescription of those services delegated to the agent physician.

Examples of consequent coverage or reimbursement limitations that have led to inefficiencies include greater coverage of inpatient than of outpatient services, requirements of treatment in a hospital before approval of nursing home care, the higher value placed on surgical than on medical procedures irrespective of their value to the patient, limitations on reimbursement for preventive measures and education of patients, and restrictions on claims paid tied to the service rendered and to the type of provider.

The complexity of jointly optimizing care and cost requires that providers have the incentives and the ability to organize services on a dynamic functional basis—not on the static dysfunctional basis that is built into the conventional system of delivery and payment. The dynamic approach allows individual needs to be determined by outcome and quality. Its drawback lies in its potential inability to ensure that systems offering dynamic definitions of care also produce results of high quality.

Increased Assumption of Risk. For an industry whose payment methods offered very little real risk, perhaps the most striking supply-side change is the growing numbers of providers that are willing to assume some degree of financial risk for the delivery of health care services. The most prevalent form is the HMO with its various delivery models, from closed-group panel to independent practice association.

Under HMO arrangements a predetermined schedule of benefits is provided for a fixed monthly fee. This method of reimbursement counters the traditional incentives for providers to increase revenue by increasing the volume of services. As long as patients' satisfaction and the ethical issues of quality are ensured, profits are maximized by minimizing costs. The greatest savings attributed to HMOs have traditionally come through a reduction in the number of hospital days per 1,000 HMO enrollees.[24] Greater reductions in admissions have occurred in HMO plans with closer organizational structures that are able to influence practice behavior.[25] The objectives of the closed group may be in greater conformity than those of a more decentralized group. Moreover, utilization review may be enhanced as norms of practice are established and reinforced through close association.

The HMO is assuming a role that has not been well played by traditional insurers: the arranging and rearranging of health care delivery methods. At the same time, the idea of insurance is not being abridged by HMOs. Provider-operated HMOs are now being challenged by traditional insurance firms, which have moved into a more proactive "care arranger" role. Current trends in hospital occupancy rates and physician supply are contributing to the establishment of new forms of delivery and finance in which providers share risk.

Discounts Based on Exclusivity and Volume. Over the past several years, hospitals and physicians have become more willing to discount the price of their services. These arrangements have emerged as substitutes for HMOs and fee-for-service plans in some markets where efficient HMOs are not feasible or have not emerged for certain groups. They are innovative methods designed to gain a preferred position with the purchaser of medical services, such as a union or employer group, and in return offer a guaranteed potential volume to the provider.

These arrangements have been called preferred provider organizations (PPOs). Their forms are so diverse that a clear, consistent definition has not emerged. PPOs are generally far less formally structured; they do not lock the patient into any one provider for services. The incentive for individual use is a discounted price or lower copayments, usually accompanied by some form of organized utilization control.

125

Whether PPOs will thrive is uncertain. Some critics claim that they do not differ from the early Blue Cross and Blue Shield plans. What is clear is that they constitute an innovative attempt to meet the problem of shrinking financial resources for health care, with fewer restrictions on patients than occur under HMOs. They also permit direct negotiation of prices between providers and employers. It has been posited that PPOs combine the best of fee-for-service, in that consumers have freedom of choice, and the best of an HMO in that there is some built-in cost-consciousness about utilization.

There is no doubt that such initiatives are positive forces for injecting a new kind of competition into the health care field—price competition. Discounts are only one approach, one that may have little value in the long run. Without other horizontal and vertical changes that directly address cost minimization, the effect of discounts on cost control will be limited.

Dynamic Definition of Quality. The predominant mind-set of policy makers in health care has been to expand access and to improve the quality of care. The sanctity of life is a basic building block of our Judeo-Christian heritage. The preservation and promotion of life and their ethical pursuit are the basis of the Hippocratic oath. But for all their grandeur and deep meaning, these terms are relative. They are relative to what methods are available to sustain life, what quality of life is acceptable, and what resources are needed for its attainment. Through modern technology and reimbursement systems, we have achieved a highly accessible and technologically advanced health care system. Progress since World War II has been remarkable, and we are on the brink of many technological breakthroughs.

These benefits have had high costs, however, both total costs and the increasing percentage of the gross national product consumed for health care. It is these costs that have directed so much attention to cost containment, but efforts to control costs must account for their effects on quality and accessibility.

Steps toward cost reduction must be tempered by the realization that the total system comprises thousands of individuals requiring a diverse set of health care services. Given the tension between individual needs and the needs of society, providers appear to have a growing propensity to base their practice patterns on a dynamic definition of quality. Technology and appropriate incentives for providers, for example, make possible cost-effective shifts in surgical procedures from an inpatient to an outpatient setting without sacrificing quality. In 1979, 11.3 percent of surgical procedures at the Carle Foundation

126

Hospital were performed on an outpatient basis, higher than the national average for that year. By 1981 the percentage had risen to 22 percent, a 95 percent increase. Growing consumer acceptance allowed the increase to occur, but a collaborative effort by the hospital and the clinic to minimize costs permitted it to occur without the sacrifice of quality. The use of integrated services permitted comparable costs for total surgical care for the Carle population to decrease over this period.

Improved methods of quality assurance that provide more precise measures of the relation between inputs and results are permitting providers to take greater account of that relation. The trend is toward using procedures that produce the same results at less cost rather than the newest or most fashionable procedures. Whether this trend will continue depends, in large part, on whether the incentives for providers to assume this form of risk continue.

Incentives are needed in delivery and reimbursement structures that promote production efficiency based on reasonably expected outcomes. A better understanding by policy makers and consumers of the cost dynamics inherent in our traditional definition of quality would permit better definition of methods to provide those incentives. The effects of malpractice premiums and judgments on health care costs are well documented. "Defensive" medicine exists. It consists of medical practices that are primarily aimed not at outcomes of care but at outcomes of lawsuits. Its effect goes well beyond the additional tests and procedures that may be ordered. It also has effects on how and when functions and services are rendered. The current definition of quality as perfection has built-in production costs that only society, through changes in malpractice laws and attitudes, can effectively eliminate.

Supply-side approaches to these issues of cost and quality are occurring. Groups of physicians and hospitals are altering their forms of malpractice protection through provider-focused approaches such as self-insurance, captive insurance, and other cooperatives. They differ from more traditional approaches in tying membership of the individual practitioner to a commitment to monitor the quality of care, to participate in risk management, and to engage in dynamic review of practice patterns.

Hospitals and their medical staffs are scrutinizing alterations in practice privileges of physicians more than ever before, in part because of problems associated with malpractice. This reflects a concern over quality from a defensive malpractice point of view but also a growing reality: that the dynamics of physician-hospital supply are creating a need for a more formalized and responsive relationship.

Other Providers. The trends of reorganization, multi-institutional grouping, diversification, and increased emphasis on strategic planning and marketing are taking place throughout other subsystems of health care. Traditional insurance companies are becoming more like providers; equipment and supply manufacturers are coming to have greater influence on the actual delivery of care. Other professionals, such as chiropractors, are beginning to diversify into markets that were traditionally the exclusive province of allopathic physicians.

These changes have been both spurred and stunted by regulatory and other forces. Full efficiency of production within all seven subsystems of the health care delivery system shown in table 7-1 is yet to be realized. Alternative institutional care, such as extended care, and the expanded use of home care and other associated services hold great promise for further improvement in efficiency. Whether greater efficiency will slow the growth of health care costs will largely be up to the regulatory and reimbursement forces that shape the environment within which services are rendered. An environment designed to promote the public good through prudent limited regulation and a more market-oriented approach has great promise. Allowing the enormous complexity of health care delivery to be guided by these principles and the role of government as purchaser to be defined on a fair and equitable payment basis is essential. Only then can the larger social issue of who should receive how much health care be addressed in the context of a more efficient health care system.

Effects of Supply Responses on the Poor. The final question to which we wish to direct attention is, What conditions are necessary for the delivery systems discussed to render medical services efficiently to the poor? Two conditions are of concern: whether public funding will be adequate to encourage providers to enter markets serving the poor; and the stability of eligible populations. Two additional concerns are ensuring the quality of care and assessing how much society should allocate to finance care for the poor.

Because the poor do not have sufficient resources to purchase medical services, the supply of those services is often lacking or of inferior quality in poor neighborhoods even when overall supply is excessive. The absence of economic incentives has led to this limited supply. With the increased supply of doctors entering the market, more providers may be attracted to practicing in low-income areas. If the number of providers is sufficient, group practices, HMOs, and other provider configurations may enter the market to compete effectively for public expenditures and offer differentiated services to beneficiaries.

Our view of this supply response—given public funding—is one of guarded optimism. Luft's extensive review of the rise of HMOs and prepaid group plans in demonstration projects and in real world experiences suggests that prepaid plans can help to serve the poor.[26] Providers were available to participate in these arrangements in various locations throughout the country, and when regulatory problems are taken into account, they performed well.

Two considerations in public financing of care are important. Reimbursing providers at a rate that might attract significant numbers to serve Medicaid patients may have unsatisfactory cost-containment side effects for other segments of the market. Therefore, the reimbursement rate should be altered to take advantage of the configurations of supply and demand in each market area. Second, supply configurations should be viewed as dynamic, requiring time to adjust efficiently to market forces. Public policies that force supply adjustments to occur too rapidly are likely to generate inefficient responses and problems of quality control.

The second condition that must be present to design efficient risk-sharing methods of purchasing medical services for the poor is a stable eligible population. Providers are likely to be reluctant to assume a substantial share of the risks if the covered group and thus its health needs change frequently. Plans operating under these conditions are not likely to achieve significant cost savings. Plans need to segment the population to provide one method of payment for long-term recipients and another for short-term recipients.

Quality control is a growing concern as more emphasis is placed on reducing health care costs. Assessing the quality of care is difficult because of the many dimensions of quality. Clearly, the relation between treatment patterns (including the organizational structure of the providers) and medical outcomes is of great importance, yet is not precise.

Other issues arise in discussing quality. Many observers perceive that limiting the patient's choice of provider would decrease the quality of care. Yet allowing freedom of choice does not necessarily yield higher-quality care (witness the number of individuals in the private sector of the market who voluntarily restrict their choices among physicians by joining closed-panel HMOs). Clearly, quality control is not a new issue. The traditional fee-for-service retrospective payment system, by encouraging the overuse of medical services, raised quality concerns as well.

That quality controls must be built into health care policies cannot be overstated. Those controls must be explicit, however, in relating quality to health outcomes and realistic in providing adequate revenues to permit providers to cover their reasonable costs. If "under-paid" providers boycott Medicaid, for example, beneficiaries will often seek primary care in high-cost and inappropriate settings. In this case, suppression of prices leads to both false economies and an adverse effect on access to care.

Finally, and closely related to quality, society must decide how much health care is to be financed for the poor. Policy makers must make difficult choices that bring expectations and promises into balance with resources. The amount of health care available, even from an efficient configuration of suppliers, depends on adequate revenues. In areas where multiple pricing exists (for Medicare, Medicaid, and private paying patients), cost shifting may disguise and forestall the need for an answer to this question. It may even lead to tiered medical markets serving these different populations.[27] Policy makers must deal with both the economic and the moral issues of who should receive life-extending procedures and other forms of high-technology treatment that are exceedingly expensive under any delivery system.

Regardless of the answers to any of these difficult issues, the policies established should offer providers and consumers incentives to make efficient choices about health production and consumption. Flexibility for the development of integrated supply organizations must be maintained to achieve these goals.

Notes

1. Mark V. Pauly, "Paying the Piper and Calling the Tune: The Relationship between Public Financing and Public Regulation of Health Care," in Mancur Olson, ed., *A New Approach to the Economics of Health Care* (Washington, D.C.: American Enterprise Institute, 1981), pp. 67–86.

2. Richard Zeckhauser and Christopher Zook, "Failures to Control Health Costs: Departures from First Principles," in Olson, *A New Approach*, pp. 97–116.

3. Paul J. Feldstein, *Health Care Economics* (New York: John Wiley and Sons, 1979).

4. J. M. Scott, "Federal Support for Nursing Education to Improve Quality of Practice," *Public Health Reports*, vol. 94, no. 1 (1979), pp. 31–35.

5. R. M. Scheffler et al., "Physicians and New Health Practictioners: Issues of the 1980's," *Inquiry*, vol. 16 (1979), pp. 195–229.

6. American Medical Association, Center for Health Services Research and Development, *Profile of Medical Practice, 1980* (Monroe, Wis.,1980).

7. Zeckhauser and Zook, "Failures to Control."

8. Ibid.

9. C. Watts and G. Updegraff, *Regulation and Capital Expenditures* (Denver: Spectrum Research, 1975).

10. W. J. Bicknell and D. C. Walsh, "Certificate of Need: The Massachusetts

Experience," *New England Journal of Medicine,* vol. 292 (1975), pp. 1054–61.

11. Bruce Steinwald and Frank A. Sloan, "Regulatory Approaches to Hospital Cost Containment: A Synthesis of Empirical Evidence," in Olson, *A New Approach,* pp. 274-308.

12. D. S. Salkever and T. W. Bice, "The Impact of Certificate of Need Controls on Hospital Investment," *Milbank Memorial Fund Quarterly,* vol. 54, no. 2 (Spring 1975), pp. 185–214.

13. R. Douglas and R. Miller, *Economic Regulation of Domestic Air Transport* (Washington, D.C.: Brookings Institution, 1974).

14. U.S. Department of Health and Human Services, *Health, United States, 1981* (Hyattsville, Maryland, 1981).

15. Ibid.

16. J. P. Newhouse, "Toward a Theory of Non-Profit Institutions: An Economic Model of a Hospital," *American Economic Review,* vol. 60, no. 1 (1970), pp. 64–74; and Mark V. Pauly and M. Redisch, "The Not-for-Profit Hospital as a Physicians' Cooperative," *American Economic Review,* vol. 63, no. 1 (1973), pp. 87–100.

17. American Hospital Association, *Hospital Statistics* (Chicago: American Hospital Association, 1982).

18. Jack A. Meyer, *Passing the Health Care Buck: Who Pays the Hidden Costs?* (Washington, D.C.: American Enterprise Institute, 1983).

19. Ibid.

20. Department of Health and Human Services, *Health, United States, 1981.*

21. Ibid.

22. Harold S. Luft, *Health Maintenance Organizations: Dimensions of Performance* (New York: John Wiley, 1981); and R. J. Arnould, L. W. DeBrock, and J. W. Pollard, "The Effects of Health Maintenance Organizations on Health Care Markets," *Inquiry,* vol. 21 (Fall 1984), pp. 243-54.

23. R. J. Arnould and L. W. DeBrock, "A Re-examination of Medical Society Control of Blue Shield Plans," *Advances in Health and Human Services Research,* vol. 5 (forthcoming); and R. J. Arnould and D. Eisenstadt, "The Effects of Provider Controlled Blue Shield Plans: Regulatory Options," in Olson, *A New Approach.*

24. Luft, *Health Maintenance Organizations.*

25. Ibid.

26. Ibid.

27. Pauly, "Paying the Piper."

8

Changes in Certificate-of-Need Laws: Read the Fine Print

Merton D. Finkler

It is performance that counts. Phillips Petroleum keeps telling us so. When it comes to controls on medical facility costs, however, we live by no such rule. With much faith we have publicly adopted certificate-of-need (CON) review policies under the rationale "CON reduces duplication, so it must save millions." A variety of studies have provided evidence to the contrary.[1] Despite such evidence, many existing programs have been broadened to cover more medical procedures and to include more places where care might be provided. How can such phenomena be explained? Many possible routes might be taken in answering this question; this research explores hospital self-interest to explain such persistence. The results suggest that great care must be taken when evaluating changes in CON law; what appears to be a lowering may in effect be a raising of the barriers to entry. In the first four sections of this paper, I provide evidence for four major claims:

- CON review does not control the costs of hospital-delivered services.
- Hospitals use revenues from some services to pay for others that they prefer to provide but could not without the opportunity to cross-subsidize.
- Free-standing ambulatory surgical centers (FASCs) are a cost-effective alternative to hospitals for the delivery of certain services. Moreover, FASCs do not diminish and may improve the quality of patient care. (Ambulatory surgery is all surgery that does not entail an overnight stay.)
- Since tighter rate review would impinge on cross-subsidization, hospitals might support it only in exchange for raised barriers to entry for competitors (such as FASCs) or reduced barriers for themselves.

132

The 1983 law passed in Wisconsin is one example of contemporary interest.

The policy implications of this analysis are quite profound. We need to monitor changes in CON legislation carefully if competition is to play a major role in cost containment. Furthermore, since the regulatory policies of many states incorporate trade-offs not in the public interest, they need to be overhauled. I offer a few brief thoughts about such an overhaul in the final section of this paper.

CON Review Does Not Control Costs

As suggested in *Alice in Wonderland*, how to get there depends on where you want to go. Legislators have a variety of objectives in mind when they pass CON laws.[2] Those most often cited include containing costs, reducing disparity in the availability of medical service, matching services to needs on the basis of some rules of thumb, and qualifying for various federal programs. Except for Louisiana, all states either have or have had CON review programs of some sort. Some have been in effect since the mid-1960s. Wisconsin explicitly stated in its most recent law that cost containment is the primary priority; it is reasonable to suppose that the same can be said of other states.

With this priority in mind, my sole concern here is how effectively CON review contains hospital costs. A report of the National Center for Health Services Research (NCHSR) summarized the results as follows:

• CON review may have had some effect on reducing the rate of expansion of bed supply in hospitals.

• CON review has not appeared to constrain other types of hospital capital expenditure, such as that on new equipment.

• CON review may have acted as a barrier to entry for proprietary hospitals and free-standing competitors of existing hospitals.

In sum, "The 'bottom' line from empirical research is still that CON has not succeeded in cost containment."[3]

Hospitals Cross-Subsidize

This section explores how and why hospitals use the revenue from some services to subsidize others. Such an exploration requires a theory of how hospitals behave, a theory that must address two major questions: Who makes the decisions? and, What are the objectives of the decision makers? The answer to the first question must be administrators, trustees, the medical staff, consumers, or the state. Answers to the second question have included public interest, profits, prestige, maximum provision of service, and some notion of utility that encompasses one or more of these. I assume that hospitals try to maximize both the quality and the quantity of services provided.[4] This notion is consistent with observations of actual behavior and with much of the literature.

The arguments presented in this chapter seem to hold for the first three listed responses to the question, Who decides? The exceptions are the last two entries on the list. If competitive markets for each medical service existed, then consumers (as patients or as insurance holders) would have a major role. The evidence cited here suggests that price competition has not been prevalent; so consumers have not played such a role. Alternatively, if the state, through a centralized decision-making process, made the key decisions about allocating resources, then the other objectives cited would also need to be considered. Centralized decision making is not, however, a dominant feature of medical care delivery in the United States; thus one or more of the first three options must be the correct response to, Who decides?

I now turn to the two objectives. Quality refers to the ability of a hospital to perform particular services and tests. I especially have in mind those based on expensive modern technology; such services increase the prestige of a hospital. Quantity refers to the ability to provide service quickly, that is, to have sufficient capacity to avoid queues of patients.[5] I stress quality and quantity (or, more narrowly, prestige and capacity) as the central objectives since they are what attract doctors. To use Paul Ellwood's words, "Hospitals don't have patients. Hospitals have doctors, and doctors have patients. Therefore, hospitals compete for doctors."[6]

Hospitals, of course, do not have free rein in satisfying their objectives. They are constrained by a budget (however generated) or by price competition, if it exists. The opportunity cost of the trade-off between quality and quantity depends on how constraining each of these forces is. In the 1970s they were not binding. Most services were reimbursed on a retrospective cost-plus basis, and there was very little price competition between hospitals or from alternative providers. As a result, the quality of service increased at a rate higher than patients (as patients or as insurance premium payers) would have been willing to pay if given the choice. Choice was not readily available, however; there were and are barriers to entry for lower-cost/lower-technology services. Furthermore, there was little incentive to choose; reimbursement for costs after service had been provided was the norm, especially for hospital-delivered services.[7]

This quality-quantity-maximizing model helps explain two common phenomena: why internal subsidies exist and why nonprofit hospitals argue against the existence of proprietary hospitals or competitors such as free-standing ambulatory surgical centers. Although there is some debate about how to determine the amount of cross-subsidy, some services (such as outpatient departments, diagnostic and therapeutic services, X-ray departments, and laboratories) are often cited as providing revenues greater than costs, others (such as open-heart surgery and organ transplantation) as having costs much greater than revenue generated.[8] These latter services draw doctors to hospitals and thus increase the hospitals' quality (prestige). Revenues from the first set of services or from some external sources are necessary to make all this possible.

Several successful predictions bear out the strength of this approach. In particular, we find substantial duplication of services, especially of expensive equipment, among hospitals. We also find substantial excess capacity, which is consistent with the quantity objective. Finally, with the exception of nursing home care, we find that the hospital sector has had the highest growth rate of medical expenditures during the past two decades. In 1967 dollars, hospital expenditures per patient-day rose from roughly $36 in 1960 to $70 in 1970 and to $120 in 1980.[9] Two factors that help to explain this growth are the opportunities for hospitals to pass on costs to third-party payers and the lack of competition that might discourage such activity.

In the 1980s these conditions have been changing and will continue to do so. Changes in reimbursement have been the primary catalysts. A number of insurance programs now deviate markedly from retrospective cost-based reimbursement. Many states, as major purchasers of care or as rate regulators, are employing prospective reimbursement schemes, some of which make adjustments at year end while others do not. Some are applicable only to Medicaid recipients; others cover all payers. The federal government has also begun to change its reimbursement policies for Medicare and Medicaid. As of October 1983 hospital reimbursement based on a standard fee for each diagnosis-related group (DRG) became the policy objective. A third source of change has been the increasing popularity of health maintenance organizations (HMOs). Since HMOs economize on the use of hospitals, they compete with hospital-delivered care. Because each change has reduced opportunities to cross-subsidize, the trade-off between quality and quantity has become more stringent.

With these changes in mind, I can begin to broach the central concern of this chapter. Hospitals facing a changing financial environment must change their behavior. If they can still obtain positive net revenues by expanding cross-subsidizing services such as outpatient surgery and emergency treatment, they will try to do so—even if the net revenue from each case is less than it was under retrospective cost reimbursement. In 1982, for example, roughly 70 percent of all metropolitan hospitals had outpatient surgery departments.[10]

Of course, centers outside hospitals can also provide these services and, as the next section attests, may be able to do so more efficiently and effectively than hospitals can. To maintain the current quantity and quality of services, hospitals cannot allow these competitors to come into existence. This notion forms the basis for my final claim, presented below, that hospitals might support rate regulation in exchange for barriers to entry.

FASCs Are More Efficient and More Effective Than Hospitals

Free-standing ambulatory surgical centers can perform medical services more cost-effectively and more efficaciously than hospitals when given a fair opportunity to do so. Several studies of high-volume surgical procedures indicate that FASCs provide such services at less than the cost for inpatient surgery.[11] Detmer cites a comparison between outpatient departments at hospitals and FASCs; the latter provided these services at 11 percent below the cost of the former. Charges for some procedures can be as much as 60 percent less at FASCs than at hospitals.[12] Just the existence of an independently owned FASC can put pressure on hospitals to reduce their charges for outpatient surgery. A study for the Federal Trade Commission reports that a new FASC in St. Paul helped to reduce hospital charges for ambulatory surgery by 50 percent.[13]

I now turn to efficacy. A study by the Health Care Financing Administration of 900 patients in Phoenix provided the following summary of patients' testimony.

> Ambulatory surgical units consistently outperformed hospital inpatient units in terms of friendliness of staff, attention to patients' needs, pleasantness of the environment, and quality of care. Patients treated in hospital-based and free-standing ambulatory surgical units were more likely to say that they would choose the same setting again than were their inpatient counterparts.
>
> Patients thought they had saved time and money and were spared the emotional stress associated with hospitalization.[14]

In addition, physicians reported that they preferred FASCs to hospital outpatient clinics for minor surgery. Of course, one would like to know how often complications arise in FASCs. Natof found that only 106 of 13,433 FASC patients in Chicago suffered complications, 16 required hospitalization, and none had heart attacks or died.[15] Detmer suggests that 20 to 40 percent of all inpatient surgery could be done as outpatient surgery. He claims that many complications that do arise are related more to the judgment and skill of the surgeon than to the surgical setting. This would seem to hold for both hospital outpatient departments and FASCs.[16]

That FASCs are efficient and effective does not mean that they are viable everywhere. The Federal Trade Commission study claims that they would be viable competitors for hospitals *if* they faced the same rules and opportunities.[17] For example:

• if they were eligible for payment under part B of Medicare (this has been true only since March 1982)
• if similar insurance coverage existed (Blue Cross–Blue Shield is slowly changing what it reimburses; Medicare has recently expanded its coverage to include both professional fees and some overhead costs)
• if licensing and CON review did not differ between FASCs and hospitals (in Wisconsin they do, see next section)[18]
• if Blue Cross and Blue Shield participated (their policy differs greatly in different states).[19]

The results just cited are not the subject of great debate; however, some who argue against FASC applications claim that total costs of medical delivery systems will not be decreased by their existence. The Southeast Wisconsin Health Systems Agency argues that hospitals will increase other charges to make up for the lost business.[20] The key question we must ask is, Can they? The answer depends on how hospitals are reimbursed for services and on whether it is possible to decertify services that are not cost effective. If retrospective cost reimbursement ceases to be commonplace, hospitals must face a more difficult trade-off between quality and quantity than they have had to face in the past.[21]

Hospitals Might Support Rate Regulation in Exchange for Barriers to Entry

The preceding three sections have demonstrated that CON review has not had great success in controlling costs, that hospitals cross-subsidize services, and that free-standing ambulatory surgical centers can be effective competitors for hospitals in outpatient surgery. If hospitals are to maintain their desired quantity and quality, they cannot have competitors for those services that generate net revenue. They would thus like to raise the barriers to entry for such competitors, and CON review provides an opportunity to do so. The evidence presented below is consistent with the notion that hospitals will be willing participants in the rate regulation process if they can obtain legislative approval for raising such entry barriers.

If a rate review commission's concern were solely with cost containment, it would encourage substitution of care in a less costly setting (such as a physician's office, an FASC, or a patient's home) for care in a hospital. Feldstein claims (and the Wisconsin Health Systems Agency—as reflected by the Rode report—corroborates) that these commissions are interested in the survival of existing hospitals. Furthermore, the evidence in medical care delivery is similar to that for the airline and trucking industries, where rate regulation went hand in hand with entry barriers for new firms.[22]

Alternative views exist, of course, about why hospitals support rate regulation. One often cited rationale goes as follows.[23] If an independent rate-regulating commission were to prescribe rates for all payers, a hospital's ability to predict its financial future would be improved. Furthermore, if equal payment were to come from all bill payers (Medicare, Medicaid, Blue Cross), there would be little need to shift costs among third parties or between insured and self-paying patients.[24] Of course, various bases might be employed for determining payment (such as per episode or per patient-day), and each reimbursement mechanism would offer a different incentive. Without investigation of specific policies, it is not possible to claim that rate regulation would be supported by hospitals. It is also not clear that such support would exist if entry at costs below the reimbursement amount were feasible for hospital competitors.

Let us first consider those states that have mandatory rate regulation and ask how many free-standing ambulatory surgical centers they had in March 1982.[25]

State	Number of FASCs
Connecticut	6
Maryland	1
Massachusetts	0
New Jersey	5
New York	1
Rhode Island	3
Washington	3
Wisconsin	1

Now let us look at the states with the greatest number of FASCs. With the exception of Illinois, these states had either no rate regulations or voluntary ones. The number of FASCs is clearly greater than in the states with mandatory regulation (either on an absolute or on a per resident basis).[26]

State	Number of FASCs
Arizona	13
California	36
Florida	14
Illinois	47
Texas	26

Since these data reflect developments at various times, we cannot say whether a trade in fact took place. These data are, however, certainly consistent with the hypothesis that rate regulation and higher entry barriers for FASCs went hand in hand. Further analysis would be needed to ascertain whether a causal relationship exists here.

I now wish to turn to the most recent changes in Wisconsin's medical care regulatory law, where a trade-off is evident. Two major changes in the 1983 Wisconsin law are of interest. The state legislature established a hospital rate regulation commission and at the same time modified the certificate-of-need review law. Three new aspects of the CON law are pertinent:

• The main objective of the CON program is clearly stated to be cost containment and not need determination, improved quality or access, or anything else.[27]

• Construction or operation of any ambulatory surgical center must be reviewed without regard to the dollar amount of the project. Only home health agencies have been subjected to a similar status.

• The threshold level for review of other projects is either $500,000 of revenue generation for a new service or $600,000 if new equipment or beds are to be purchased. These levels have risen from $150,000 in the previous law.

Consider each of these changes. It is not clear how the first change will be implemented. The Wisconsin Department of Health and Social Services is studying its implementation, and a moratorium on CON applications is in existence while it does. The second change clearly makes it more difficult for FASCs to come into existence. Previous law listed ambulatory surgery as one of eight procedures that would require CON review if the $150,000 threshold were surpassed, but FASCs were not separately distinguished as they are under present law. The third change allows more capital expenditures to take place without review except for FASCs and home health agencies. These changes surely discourage some constructive competitive responses to the inflation of hospital costs.

Policy Implications

In the end, we are left with the 1983 Wisconsin CON law and existing laws in a number of other states that discourage some particularly fruitful forms of competition. I have focused on free-standing ambulatory surgical centers, but similar arguments should be explored for free-standing emergency centers or home health agencies. Existing law in many states places very high barriers in front of new entrants and thus thwarts one aspect of competitive strategies for reducing hospital cost inflation. This result may be neither an oversight nor a mistake by legislators; it just might be the consequence of a trade made with hospitals in exchange for their cooperation in a mandatory rate regulation process. Recent data are consistent with this notion, since states with mandatory rate regulation have few if any FASCs, and the states with the most FASCs have voluntary or nonexistent rate regulation.[28]

As an alternative to CON review and rate regulation, legislators should consider policies that split off some services now provided by hospitals. Such a strategy would mean decertifying certain services and perhaps closing some hospitals, but consumers as patients and as payers of insurance premiums would benefit. Of course, the existence of scale economies and of desired subsidies must be considered in implementing such an approach. These considerations entail cost-benefit analysis. If it is determined that a subsidy is in order or that external funding is desirable, policy makers should carefully assess where that subsidy is to come from and to whom it should go. Such subsidies now arise from group insurance premiums, payroll taxes, or charges paid directly for medical services. They are neither efficient nor equitable; the appropriate means of subsidizing should be consciously decided by states or the federal government. The decision should address the question of whether the purpose is income redistribution or improved efficiency. Public finance economists have devoted substantial attention to this problem.[29]

CON laws are changing in many states, as is the rhetoric concerning procompetitive proposals, but rhetoric is not a substitute for good content. Changes such as the most recent reform of Wisconsin's certificate-of-need law fail to address the real issues.

Notes

1. See, for example, Frank A. Sloan, "Government and the Regulation of Hospital Care," *American Economic Review* (May 1982), pp. 196–202; and National Center for Health Services Research (NCHSR), *A Synthesis of Research on Competition in the Financing and Delivery of Health Service*, U.S. Department of Health and Human Services, 1982.

2. For a full discussion of these objectives, see Policy Analysis—Urban Systems, *Evaluation of the Effects of Certificate of Need Programs*, Final Report, Bureau of Health Planning, August 1980.

3. NCHSR, *Synthesis of Research*, p. 21. For further discussion of how such conclusions were reached, see Sloan, "Government and Regulation of Hospital Care"; and Bruce Steinwald and Frank A. Sloan, "Regulatory Approaches to Hospital Cost Containment: A Synthesis of the Empirical Evidence," in Mancur Olson, ed., *A New Approach to the Economics of Health Care* (Washington, D.C.: American Enterprise Institute, 1981).

4. For a comprehensive discussion of hospital behavior, see Paul Feldstein, *Health Care Economics*, 2d ed. (New York: John Wiley and Sons, 1983), or Karen Davis, "Economic Theories of Behavior on Non-profit, Private Hospitals," *Economic and Business Bulletin*, vol. 24 (Winter 1972), pp. 1–13.

5. This notion of quantity is based on Jeffrey E. Harris, "The Internal Organization of Hospitals: Some Economic Implications," *Bell Journal of Economics* (Autumn 1977), pp. 467–82. It treats hospitals and medical staff as two firms that jointly determine the supply of and the demand for hospital services. If hospitals wish to attract doctors, they want to make sure the delay in providing service to their patients is as short as possible. Of course, this is distinctly different from a national health service such as that provided in England, where queues for nonemergency care are legend.

6. See Alain Enthoven, *Health Plan* (Reading, Mass.: Addison-Wesley, 1980).

7. The NCHSR (*A Synthesis of Research*) reports that roughly 90 percent of all hospital expenditures were covered by third-party payment. For a more detailed presentation of this argument, see Feldstein, *Health Care Economics*, chaps. 10 and 11.

8. For some discussion of examples, see William A. Glaser, "Paying the Hospital: Foreign Lessons for the United States," *Health Care Financing Review* (Summer 1983), pp. 99–110, and Jeffrey E. Harris, "Pricing Rules for Hospitals," *Bell Journal of Economics* (Spring 1979), pp. 224–43. What is and what is not cross-subsidized is not perfectly clear, but as suggested by Mark V. Pauly and Kathryn M. Langwell ("Research on Competition in the Financing and Delivery of Health Services: Future Research Needs," NCHSR Research Proceedings Series, U.S. Department of Health and Human Services, October 1982), the topic deserves more attention than it has received. One major problem is how to differentiate between charges, accounting costs, and the true marginal costs of providing services. See Steven A. Finkler, "The Distinction between Costs and Charges," *Annals of Internal Medicine*, vol. 96 (January 1982), pp. 102–9.

9. The data come from Robert M. Gibson, "National Health Expenditures, 1979," *Health Care Financing Review* (Summer 1980), pp. 1–36. Explanations for the inflation of hospital costs can be found in Karen Davis, "Theories of Hospital Inflation: Some Empirical Evidence," *Journal of Human Resources*, vol. 8 (Spring 1973), pp. 181–201, and in Feldstein, *Health Care Economics*.

10. These data come from American Hospital Association, *Hospital Statistics*, 1983. Previous issues of this publication allow us to trace a rapid rate of growth in outpatient departments at community hospitals. In 1970 only in eight states was the percentage of hospitals with outpatient departments greater than 50 percent, and only in fifteen states was it greater than 40 percent. By 1982 these departments existed in at least 50 percent of the hospitals in seventeen states and more than 40 percent in thirty-one states.

11. See Don E. Detmer, "Ambulatory Surgery," *New England Journal of Medicine* (December 1981), pp. 1406–9, and Michael Rode, J. Michael Funkhauser, and Leslie Taylor, "Free Standing Ambulatory Surgical Centers: A White Paper Report," Southeast Wisconsin Health Systems Agency, March 1983.

12. Rode et al. ("Free Standing Ambulatory Surgical Centers") cite a comparison of average charges for sixteen procedures at seven hospitals and nine FASCs in the Midwest. For three services, FASC charges were less than half hospital charges; for nine other procedures, FASC charges were at least 25 percent below hospital charges. For only two procedures did hospitals report lower charges. Numerous other surveys report similar results. James Wolff and Dale R. Dunnihoo, "A Free-standing Ambulatory Surgical Unit: A Success of Failure?" *Journal of Obstetrics and Gynecology* (1982), pp. 270–76, and several respondents provide evidence supporting the claim that FASCs are less costly and much more convenient for both doctors and patients than either inpatient or outpatient hospitals and at least as safe, especially for two commonly performed surgical procedures—curettage and laparoscopy. Furthermore, Wolff and Dunnihoo report that the charge per patient for these procedures when performed in an FASC fell by 25 percent between 1978 and 1981. This is in stark contrast with virtually every other medical service provided. Of course, charge accounting and cost accounting are not the same thing (see note 8).

13. See Joan B. Trauner, Harold S. Luft, and Joy O. Robinson, *Entrepreneurial Trends in Health Care Delivery*, Federal Trade Commission, 1982, chap. 5.

14. Detmer, "Ambulatory Surgery," p. 1407.

15. Herbert E. Natof, "Complications Associated with Ambulatory Surgery," *Journal of the American Medical Association*, vol. 244 (1980), pp. 1116–18.

16. Detmer, "Ambulatory Surgery." Wolff and Dunnihoo, "A Free-standing Ambulatory Surgical Unit," report that in their study of 5,369 patients in Louisiana, patients at FASCs had an infection rate of 0.06 percent and a hospital transfer rate of 0.04 percent. They claim that morbidity and mortality rates are actually lower at FASCs than in hospitals. Of course, they note that key differences in patients' conditions may not have been taken into account. Nonetheless, these results are consistent with findings of several other surveys they cite.

17. See Trauner et al., *Entrepreneurial Trends in Health Care Delivery*.

18. Differences in the applicability of such laws have been the subject of much debate. The argument here is consistent with the economic theory of regulation that suggests that existing providers receive preferential treatment from regulators. For evidence in hospital services as well as for other sectors of the economy, see Feldstein, *Health Care Economics*, pp. 262–79.

19. At the end of 1982, Blue Cross plans provided benefits for surgery at an FASC in sixty-one of eighty districts in the United States. Of the nineteen plans that did not provide coverage, eleven reported that no FASC existed in their district. Most of these plans covered areas in the eastern states. Blue Cross and Blue Shield do cover ambulatory surgery in hospital outpatient departments in all eighty districts.

20. Rode et al., "Free Standing Ambulatory Surgical Centers."

21. We assume that prospective reimbursement will not have a complete end-of-year adjustment for costs; otherwise it would generate results quite similar to those of retrospective reimbursement.

22. Feldstein, *Health Care Economics*.

23. See Katherine G. Bauer, "Hospital Rate Setting—This Way to Salvation," *Milbank Memorial Fund Quarterly: Health and Society* (Winter 1977), pp. 117–58.

24. See Jack A. Meyer, *Passing the Health Care Buck: Who Pays the Hidden Cost?* (Washington, D.C.: American Enterprise Institute, 1983), for documentation of this phenomenon.

25. Rate regulation categories were taken from Frank A. Sloan, "Rate Regulation as a Strategy for Hospital Cost Control: Evidence from the Last Decade," *Milbank Memorial Fund Quarterly: Health and Society* (1983), pp. 195–221. Illinois, though listed as a state with mandatory rate regulation, had not implemented a program; so it is not considered in this category. The data on FASCs come from Trauner et al., *Entrepreneurial Trends in Health Care Delivery.*

26. Three of the FASCs listed for Florida and Texas were pending at the time of the Trauner study.

27. See section 150.69 of Act 27 of the 1983 Wisconsin legislature.

28. One useful extension of this study would be a state-by-state historical analysis of when CON changes and rate regulation changes took place. Our analysis would predict that many of these changes took place simultaneously.

29. Peggy B. Musgrave and Richard A. Musgrave, *Public Finance in Theory and Practice*, 4th ed. (New York: McGraw-Hill, 1984).

9

Factors Affecting the Adoption of Prospective Reimbursement Programs by State Governments

Philip Fanara, Jr., and Warren Greenberg

George Stigler, a Nobel laureate in economics, was the first to examine, with modern economic tools, the nature of economic regulation in the economy.[1] Economic regulation—licensure requirements for professionals, price supports for agriculture, tariffs and quotas on imported goods, prospective reimbursement of hospitals—pervades our entire economy.

In his seminal article Stigler suggested that regulation is no different from any other commodity bought and sold in the marketplace. It might be demanded by firms to control entry, to discourage demand for substitute commodities, or to fix prices. Both the airline industry and the trucking industry, for example, have used the power of the U.S. government to limit entry and fix prices. Moreover, according to Stigler, state legislatures are willing to award or supply regulation in return for votes, campaign contributions, or employment for party workers.[2]

Stigler's analysis of regulation has been formalized by Sam Peltzman, who suggests that the demand for regulation is determined by the magnitude of the potential net wealth transferred to the regulated.[3] Net wealth is defined as wealth minus any organization costs, such as funds to support the beneficiaries of regulation and funds spent in efforts to mitigate the effects of opposing voting blocs.[4] In contrast, the supply of regulation is positively related to campaign contributions to the state legislature. Thus regulation itself has a market with supply and demand curves and an equilibrium price and quantity.

In a summary of theories of economic regulation, Posner divides the theories into two main categories. First is the "public interest" theory of regulation, in which regulation is demanded by the public to correct "inefficient" or "inequitable" market outcomes, such as pollution that is a byproduct of an industrial process. Second is the "capture" theory of regulation, in which regulation exists and benefits are provided at the behest of the regulated firms, as many have suggested occurred in the airline and trucking industries before deregulation.[5]

In this chapter we seek to explain the demand for prospective reimbursement regulation by state governments. Prospective reimbursement is payment of the providers of health care—in particular, hospitals—on the basis of a predetermined, fixed budget. This method is a substitute for the "allowable cost" method whereby providers are reimbursed, after the fact, for any costs that fall under allowed categories.

Both the public interest and the capture theories are used in testing our hypotheses. To be more specific, since Medicaid is a line item in the state budget, among other expenditures such as education, housing, and welfare, greater outflows for Medicaid suggest lesser funds for other state programs. We hypothesize, therefore, that the greater the proportion of a state's budget that consists of expenditures for Medicaid, the greater the incentives for recipients of *other* funds in the state's budget to demand prospective reimbursement as one way of containing Medicaid expenditures. In a sense, other interests in the state have "captured" the state governments. Educators in Michigan, for example, concerned about their salaries and benefits, were some of the most vociferous lobbyists for controls of Medicaid expenditures.[6] The federal budget debates over cuts in spending for domestic programs to finance military expenditures may also be seen as a variation of the capture theory.

More formally, this version of the capture theory appears to parallel Stigler's description of the railroad industry's efforts to curtail the growth of short-haul trucks in the 1930s. In this episode, the railroads sought weight limits on trucks to limit the ability of the trucking industry to compete with the railroads.[7]

It is possible that the demand for regulation and the curtailment of Medicaid expenditures may also be derived from a public interest theory of regulation. The voters as a whole might be putting pressure on state governments to contain costs because of a perceived diminishing marginal utility of Medicaid expenditures in relation to other state programs. A clearer separation of the capture theory from the public interest theory would require a computation, if possible, of the marginal utility of Medicaid expenditures in relation to the marginal utility of expenditures for other state programs.

In addition to our hypothesis about the proportion of a state's budget for Medicaid, we also posit a pure capture theory of regulation. We hypothesize that mandatory prospective reimbursement will be adopted the greater the market share (in number of beds) of non-profit hospitals in relation to for-profit hospitals. Nonprofit hospitals might welcome regulation as protection from for-profit hospitals, which have expanded aggressively in recent years. Prospective reimbursement regulation, by allowing only formula- or budget-based increases in revenues, might freeze the market shares of the for-profit hospitals. Thus the higher the market share of the nonprofit in relation to the for-profit hospitals, the relatively greater political strength the nonprofit hospitals might exert to bring about prospective reimbursement. Moreover, one study has shown that the ratio of total revenue to total expenses in nonprofit hospitals (a proxy for profits) was unaffected by mandatory prospective reimbursement regulation.[8] Thus it seems that prospective reimbursement programs may protect nonprofit hospitals from competition without damaging their financial position.

In the next section we introduce our model of the demand for prospective reimbursement. In the third section we assess the empirical results and implications of the model. Our empirical results support our main hypothesis that the greater the percentage of a state's budget that consists of Medicaid payments, the more likely it is that mandatory prospective reimbursement will take place in that state. Our subsidiary hypothesis—that the greater the proportion of for-profit hospital beds in a state, the less likely is mandatory prospective reimbursement—is also confirmed by the empirical work. Our fourth section relates the theory of the demand for prospective reimbursement in the public sector to cost containment initiatives in the private sector. Finally, we briefly examine two additional issues in the economic theory of regulation and summarize our conclusions.

Model of Demand for Prospective Reimbursement

A number of recent studies have shown substantial cost savings from mandatory state-sponsored prospective reimbursement programs. In an examination of nine state prospective reimbursement mechanisms, Coelen and Sullivan found that prospective reimbursement can be effective in controlling hospital costs.[9] Furthermore, they suggest that mandatory prospective reimbursement programs are more consistently significantly related to reduced hospital costs than voluntary programs.[10] In his analysis of a number of state prospective reimbursement systems, Hellinger found that downstate New York hospitals have experienced reduced hospital costs per patient-day because of such programs.[11]

A recent study by Sloan examined the effects on hospital costs of regulation of the expansion of facilities and services, the economic stabilization program, and prospective reimbursement.[12] Like Coelen and Sullivan, Sloan presents evidence that "mature" mandatory prospective reimbursement programs have been significant in reducing hospital costs.[13] Joskow's extensive analysis of prospective reimbursement programs lends additional support to Sloan's conclusions.[14] Some recent work, however, suggests that favorable effects of prospective payment programs on hospital costs are limited to one or two states and that studies that aggregate all the prospective reimbursement states mask substantial differences among states in program effects.

Approximately thirty prospective reimbursement programs are operated by state agencies, Blue Cross plans, or state hospital associations.[15] And in March 1983 the Congress enacted a Reagan administration proposal establishing a system of prospective payment, based on diagnosis-related groups (DRGs), for Medicare beneficiaries.[16]

Regardless of the relative merits of prospective reimbursement, it is not known why prospective reimbursement systems are adopted in some states and not in others. Sloan originally raised this question when he asked, "Why have some states been able to enact cost-reducing programs?" Sloan further questioned "whether the experience of some states can be replicated elsewhere."[17]

By 1977 nine states had adopted mandatory prospective reimbursement systems (table 9-1). Although the mechanics, such as formula- or budget-based systems, varied, they were all mandatory programs.[18]

To test the effect on the adoption of mandatory state prospective reimbursement plans of the percentage of a state's budget made up of Medicaid payments and the proportion of a state's hospital beds in for-profit hospitals, we used the following model. Since our dependent variable is dichotomous—that is, states with or without prospective reimbursement—multiple probit and logit regression techniques were used. The maximum likelihood method was used to estimate the parameters of both models.

$$MPR = f(MP, FPB, \Delta HC, \%U, BCMS)$$

where, $MPR = 0$ for a state without mandatory prospective reimbursement, and $MPR = 1$ for a state with mandatory prospective reimbursement; MP = Medicaid payments as a percentage of a state's budget; FPB = for-profit hospital beds as a percentage of total hospital beds in the state; ΔHC = relative change in hospital costs per admission over a two-year period; $\%U$ = percent unionization in the state;

TABLE 9-1
STATES WITH MANDATORY PROSPECTIVE
REIMBURSEMENT PROGRAMS, 1977

State	Inception Date
Colorado	1977
Connecticut	1974
Maryland	1973
Massachusetts	1971
New Jersey	1971
New York	1969
Rhode Island	1971
Washington	1973
Wisconsin	1975

SOURCE: Paul Joskow, *Controlling Hospital Costs: The Role of Government Regulation* (Cambridge, Mass.: MIT Press, 1981).

and *BCMS* = Blue Cross market share in the state.[19]

Our sample consists of forty-two states and the District of Columbia. Eight states that have had Blue Cross prospective reimbursement programs were excluded since their inclusion would be a source of simultaneity bias in the regression equation.[20] Prospective reimbursement by Blue Cross may affect a state's adoption of its own mandatory prospective reimbursement program. Conversely, a state prospective reimbursement system would affect the propensity of Blue Cross to adopt such a program. Theoretically, even in qualitative choice models, such simultaneity could be solved. This problem becomes quite difficult to solve here, however, since a perceived threat of regulation is nearly impossible to measure. In addition, differences in the years when prospective reimbursement was adopted by the states used in the study and the states with Blue Cross prospective reimbursement will not allow a solution.

Our sample includes data for each of our variables for the year before the inception of prospective reimbursement. Our assumption was that there would be at least a one-year delay before a state legislature could enact prospective reimbursement legislation. For the variable "change in hospital costs per admission," the data are for two years before the date of inception. In those states without prospective reimbursement legislation, date were collected for 1972, the year before the average of the inception dates of the states with prospective reimbursement programs. Data for state Medicaid payments were not

148

available for all the states for the year before the inception of prospective reimbursement. Therefore, for the variable "state Medicaid payments as a percentage of the total state budget," the year 1972 was used for all states.

Our primary interest lies in the coefficient for Medicaid expenditures as a percentage of a state's budget (MP), for which a positive sign is predicted. Our second variable, percentage of for-profit beds in a state (FPB), would suggest a negative sign. Additional variables are introduced to increase the explanatory power of the model. We would expect the change in hospital costs per admission (ΔHC) to have a positive sign. The greater the increase in hospital costs, the greater the pressure on the state from employers and employees in the private sector to contain hospital costs. The percentage of the labor force unionized in the state ($\%U$) attempts to hold constant the political persuasion of those enacting mandatory state prospective reimbursement systems. Since a high degree of unionization might occur in a state with a greater tolerance for government regulation (and, therefore, make the state more likely to enact regulatory prospective reimbursement), a positive sign is expected.

Finally, we relate the size of the Blue Cross market share ($BCMS$), to the adoption of mandatory prospective reimbursement. A larger Blue Cross market share has been associated with a larger Blue Cross discount.[21] Under mandatory prospective reimbursement schemes, the Blue Cross discount may be abrogated, placing Blue Cross on the same competitive footing as the commercial insurers. Thus the higher the Blue Cross market share, the greater the probability that Blue Cross would oppose prospective reimbursement. Similarly, the smaller the market shares of the commercial insurers, the less market power they may have over hospitals. Consequently, the more likely they will be to support prospective reimbursement, putting all insurers on an equal payment basis. If political strengths are related to market share, the greater the Blue Cross market share, the less likely that prospective reimbursement will be adopted.

Assessing the Empirical Results

Table 9–2, columns 1 and 2, gives the results of the full probit and logit models. Each of the variables except Blue Cross market share has the predicted positive or negative sign. The Blue Cross market share has a positive sign, but its t-value is nonsignificant. T-values are reported in parentheses; however, since a maximum likelihood estimation technique was used and the number of observations was relatively small, t-values can be misleading. Therefore, hypotheses testing on each

149

TABLE 9–2
PROBIT AND LOGIT ESTIMATES FOR THE DEMAND FOR
PROSPECTIVE REIMBURSEMENT, MODELS A AND B

Variable	Probit Model A	Logit Model B
MP	.689 (1.64)	1.19 (1.52)
FPB	−.226 (−1.55)	−.379 (−1.47)
ΔHC	.008 (1.75)	.014 (1.71)
%U	.043 (.820)	.079 (.756)
BCMS	.004 (.166)	.012 (.224)
Constant	−4.73 (−2.59)	−8.4077 (−2.33)
Overall χ^2	29.9	29.5
McFadden's R^2	.68	.67

NOTE: T-values in parentheses.

TABLE 9–3
CHI-SQUARE VALUES OF THE DEMAND FOR
PROSPECTIVE REIMBURSEMENT, MODELS A AND B

Variable	Probit χ^2 value	Significance level	Logit χ^2 value	Significance level
MP	4.61	.05	3.72	.05
FPB	4.22	.05	4.29	.05
ΔHC	4.33	.05	4.33	.05
%U	.689	.75	.607	.75
BCMS	.027	.9	.049	.9

variable was interpreted in terms of the likelihood ratio. The likelihood ratio test was as follows:

$$LRT = 2\left[\ln(\hat{\beta}_{ML}) - \ln(\hat{\beta}_{CMI})\right]$$

where $LRT \sim \chi_q^2$ is a chi-square distribution with q degrees of freedom and q is equal to the number of restrictions.

The χ^2 values for testing the restriction that the coefficient of each individual variable is equal to zero appear in table 9-3. The results indicate that Medicaid as a percentage of the state budget (MP), for-profit beds as a percentage of total beds (FPB), and the change in hospital costs are statistically significant at the 5 percent level.

Table 9-4 shows the probit and logit models C and D, which were computed with only the three significant variables. Table 9-5 contains the results of the chi-square test on these variables. Comparing table 9-4 with table 9-2 reveals no significant differences in the overall chi-square value or in the McFadden R^2 value when the nonsignificant variables are eliminated.

Applicability to the Private Sector

Thus far we have analyzed the demand for mandatory prospective reimbursement in the public sector. One would expect, however, that as costs of health care insurance premiums become an increasingly greater share of the employee's wage and benefit package, employers might begin, with their employees' consent, to seek a wage-benefit package with greater emphasis on cost containment.[22]

The recent increases in corporate initiatives in health care, such as the formation of business coalitions, the establishment of alternative delivery systems, and greater use of copayments and deductibles, may have come about because of corporate examination of increased health care premiums in relation to salaries and wages.[23] Samors and Sullivan also suggest that private sector initiatives originate in corporations such as the Ford Motor Company and the Caterpillar Tractor Company that have experienced "soaring costs of providing employee health benefits." Samors and Sullivan further relate that "Ford Motor Company's health costs, for instance, rose from $68 million in 1965 to $650 million in 1981, doubling roughly every five years. Health costs for Caterpillar Tractor Company grew from $65 million in 1975 to $146 million in 1981. This growth does not reflect an increase in the number of employees covered nor in benefits offered."[24]

Additional research is needed on the statistically significant factors associated with a firm's adoption of a cost containment strategy in health care.

TABLE 9–4

PROBIT AND LOGIT ESTIMATES FOR THE DEMAND FOR
PROSPECTIVE REIMBURSEMENT, MODELS C AND D

Variable	Probit Model C	Logit Model D
MP	.87 (2.38)	1.54 (2.24)
FPB	−.24 (−2.05)	−.42 (−1.96)
ΔHC	.008 (1.90)	.01 (1.83)
Constant	−3.96 (−2.85)	−6.95 (−2.63)
Overall χ^2	29.22	28.86
McFadden's R^2	.66	.65

NOTE: T-values in parentheses.

TABLE 9–5

CHI-SQUARE VALUES OF THE DEMAND FOR
PROSPECTIVE REIMBURSEMENT, MODELS C AND D

Variable	Probit χ^2 value	Probit Significance level	Logit χ^2 value	Logit Significance level
MP	17.49	.005	17.46	.005
FPB	11.53	.005	11.77	.005
ΔHC	7.09	.01	7.22	.01

Two Additional Tasks in the Economic Theory of Regulation

The first task that Stigler assigned to researchers of the theory of economic regulation is to analyze the demand for regulation in an industry; the second is to ascertain which form regulation will take in an industry. This question may be asked of government regulation in the health care industry as well. That is, why was mandatory prospective reimbursement used in the nine states considered rather than limiting the scope of mandatory services, establishing case management arrangements with networks of primary care physicians, offering prepaid health plans, restricting Medicaid recipients to specific health facilities, or other forms of cost containment, such as those discussed in the AEI volume *Market Reforms in Health Care*, particularly in the Gibson paper?[25]

The second task is not a subject of this chapter, but two possible reasons why prospective reimbursement has been used as a cost containment technique in addition to the public interest and capture theories described above are that (1) prospective reimbursement mechanisms have been tested and used in foreign countries[26] and (2) some evidence exists that prospective reimbursement has achieved at least modest gains in cost containment.[27]

A third task that Stigler challenged the theorists of economic regulation to undertake is to examine the effect of regulation on the allocation of resources. To our knowledge, no economist has yet even attempted to answer this question. Most studies have concerned themselves with the effects of prospective reimbursement on rising health care costs, but this question, of course, does not at all address the issue of allocative efficiency. To address that issue, one needs to measure the divergence of the rate paid to hospitals under a prospective reimbursement system from the marginal cost of health services in the hospital.

Conclusions

In view of the increasing use of mandatory prospective reimbursement systems and the empirical evidence of their success in containing hospital costs, this study sought to gain a better understanding of the factors underlying the demand for prospective reimbursement regulation. Our study was a modest beginning since only a single model was tested, but we believe the results can provide some much needed insight into why regulation occurs or does not occur in the hospital sector.

It appears, first, that states may be concerned with their budgets and the percentage of those budgets that consists of Medicaid expenditures. Further analysis is needed to understand why this is so, but funds spent for Medicaid mean less money for other beneficiaries of the state. Although the variable reflecting change in hospital costs per admission includes all hospital costs, it is reasonable to assume that large changes in hospital costs include large changes in Medicaid payments as well. This would also create pressure on the state to limit Medicaid expenditures.

Second, the inverse relation between the percentage of for-profit hospital beds in a state and mandatory prospective reimbursement indicates that the demand for prospective reimbursement may also be derived from those who might be affected by it. Further examination is needed of the incentives of nonprofit and for-profit hospitals.

Our results should be carefully interpreted in the light of assumptions about the time period used and the small number of states that have adopted mandatory prospective reimbursement. An examination of the demand for programs such as Blue Cross prospective reimbursement in the private sector and of the demand for other public sector cost containment programs would, we believe, be a helpful complement to this research.

Finally, we are, of course, nowhere near an understanding of why some, rather than other, cost containment programs are used by states; nor has anyone even attempted to inquire what effect prospective reimbursement regulation will have on the allocation of resources. These issues need to be addressed.

Notes

1. George J. Stigler, "The Theory of Economic Regulation," *Bell Journal of Economics and Management Science* (Spring 1971), pp. 3–21.

2. Ibid., pp. 11–12.

3. Sam Peltzman, "Toward a More General Theory of Regulation," *Journal of Law and Economics* (August 1976), pp. 211–40.

4. Ibid., p. 215.

5. Richard A. Posner, "Theories of Economic Regulation," *Bell Journal of Economics and Management Science* (Autumn 1974), pp. 335–58.

6. Conversation with Rosemary Gibson, American Enterprise Institute, January 1983. See also Rosemary Gibson, "Quiet Revolutions in Medicaid," in Jack A. Meyer, ed., *Market Reforms in Health Care* (Washington, D.C.: American Enterprise Institute, 1982), p. 91.

7. Stigler, "Theory of Economic Regulation, p. 8.

8. Frank A. Sloan, "Regulation and the Rising Cost of Hospital Care," *Review of Economics and Statistics* (November 1981), pp. 484–85.

9. Craig Coelen and Daniel Sullivan, "An Analysis of the Effects of Prospective Reimbursement Programs on Hospital Expenditures," *Health Care Financing Review* (Winter 1981), p. 18.

10. Ibid.

11. Fred J. Hellinger, "An Empirical Analysis of Several Prospective Reimbursement Systems," in *Hospital Cost Containment: Selected Notes for Future Policy*, Michael Zubkoff, Ira E. Ruskin, and Ruth S. Hanft, eds. (New York:

PRODIST 1978), p. 391.

12. Sloan, "Regulation and the Rising Cost," pp. 479–87.

13. Ibid., p. 487.

14. Paul Joskow, *Controlling Hospital Costs: The Role of Government Regulation* (Cambridge, Mass.: MIT Press, 1981).

15. Coelen and Sullivan, "Analysis of the Effects," p. 1.

16. "Schweiker Confirms New DRG-based Proposal," *Washington Report on Medicine and Health*, October 11, 1982, p. 1.

17. Sloan, "Regulation and the Rising Cost," p. 487.

18. According to Joskow (*Controlling Hospital Costs*, p. 115), Rhode Island is considered a state with mandatory prospective reimbursement by the Department of Health and Human Services although its program is a cooperative among the state, the hospital association, and Blue Cross. Blue Cross as well as Medicaid reimbursement is contingent on hospital participation, and as a consequence each hospital in the state is covered by the program.

19. Obtaining some of the variables in this model and subsequent models required substantial research. Sources of the data were as follows: Data on hospital beds were obtained from American Hospital Association, *Hospital Statistics* (Chicago, various issues). Data on percent unionization and state budgets were obtained from U.S. Bureau of the Census, *Statistical Abstract of the United States*, various issues. Data on Medicaid payments by state were obtained from U.S. Department of Health, Education and Welfare, "Funds by Source Expended for Public Assistance Payment and for Administration Services and Training," December 1972. Blue Cross market share data were computed by dividing the total number of enrollees in Blue Cross plans by the number of persons insured for hospital expenses. The total number of Blue Cross enrollees was taken from Blue Cross and Blue Shield Association, *Fact Book*, various issues, 1969–1976. The total number of persons insured for hospital expenses came from Health Insurance Association of America, *Source Book of Health Insurance Data* (New York, various issues).

20. The excluded states were Delaware, Indiana, Kentucky, Michigan, Missouri, Montana, New Hampshire, and Ohio.

21. Roger Feldman and Warren Greenberg, "The Relationship between Blue Cross Market Share and Blue Cross Discount on Hospital Charges," *Journal of Risk and Insurance* (June 1981), pp. 235–46.

22. Feldman and Greenberg found, however, that between 1974 and 1977 the use of prospective reimbursement by Blue Cross in the private sector was not significantly related to the percentage increase in hospital claims expense in the state in which the plan was located. This may have been due, in part, to the probable multicollinearity between the percentage increase in hospital claims expense and the variable, mandatory state prospective reimbursement. See Roger Feldman and Warren Greenberg, "Blue Cross Market Share, Economies of Scale, and Cost Containment Efforts," *Health Services Research* (Summer 1981), pp. 175–83.

23. See John K. Iglehart, "Health Care and American Business," *New England Journal of Medicine* (January 1982), pp. 120–24.

24. Patricia W. Samors and Sean Sullivan, "Health Care Cost Containment

through Private Sector Initiatives," in Meyer, *Market Reforms in Health Care,* p. 144.

25. Gibson, "Quiet Revolutions," pp. 83, 84, 87, 90.

26. Uwe Reinhardt, "Health Insurance and Cost Containment Policies: The Experience Abroad," *American Economic Review* (May 1980), pp. 149–56.

27. Sloan, "Regulation and the Rising Cost," pp. 479–87.

28. See, for example, Clark C. Havighurst, ed., *Regulating Health Facilities Construction* (Washington, D.C.: American Enterprise Institute, 1974).

A NOTE ON THE BOOK

This book was edited by
Gertrude Kaplan and Donna Spitler.
Sally Janin designed the cover,
and Hördur Karlsson drew the figures.
The text was set in Palatino, a typeface designed by Hermann Zapf.
Hendricks-Miller Typographic Company, of Washington, D.C.,
set the type, and R. R. Donnelley & Sons Company,
of Harrisonburg, Virginia, printed and bound the book,
using permanent, acid-free paper made by the S. D. Warren Company.

AEI ASSOCIATES PROGRAM

The American Enterprise Institute invites your participation in the competition of ideas through its AEI Associates Program. This program has two objectives: (1) to extend public familiarity with contemporary issues; and (2) to increase research on these issues and disseminate the results to policy makers, the academic community, journalists, and others who help shape public policies. The areas studied by AEI include Èconomic Policy, Education Policy, Energy Policy, Fiscal Policy, Government Regulation, Health Policy, International Programs, Legal Policy, National Defense Studies, Political and Social Processes, and Religion, Philosophy, and Public Policy. For the $49 annual fee, Associates receive

- a subscription to *Memorandum*, the newsletter on all AEI activities
- the AEI publications catalog and all supplements
- a 30 percent discount on all AEI books
- a 40 percent discount for certain seminars on key issues
- subscriptions to any two of the following publications: *Public Opinion*, a bimonthly magazine exploring trends and implications of public opinion on social and public policy questions; *Regulation*, a bimonthly journal examining all aspects of government regulation of society; and *AEI Economist*, a monthly newsletter analyzing current economic issues and evaluating future trends (or for all three publications, send an additional $12).

Call 202/862-6446 or write: AMERICAN ENTERPRISE INSTITUTE
1150 Seventeenth Street, N.W., Suite 301, Washington, D.C. 20036

Managing Health Care Costs: Private Sector Innovations

SEAN SULLIVAN
with Polly M. Ehrenhaft

This volume examines little-publicized but promising private actions to slow the rise of health care costs. The first part offers four case studies—two of individual companies, Deere and Caterpillar, which have tried to gain some management control over their health care costs, and two of coalitions that have focused their members' attention on cost containment. The second part consists of a seminar in which panels discuss new models of cost containment in the private sector and the shifting of health care costs to private payers.
106 pp./1984/paper 3556-6 $7.95/cloth 3557-4 $15.95

Medicaid Reform: Four Studies of Case Management

DEBORAH A. FREUND
with Polly M. Ehrenhaft
and Marie Hackbarth

State governments across the country are taking advantage of liberalized federal rules to experiment with major reforms in their Medicaid programs. The introductory chapter of this volume describes the background of soaring health care costs and budgetary squeezes that led states to implement reforms. It then describes the common elements of the "case management" approach, which constitutes the basis of the reforms. Succeeding chapters examine in depth case management initiatives in Michigan, Kentucky, Utah, and Santa Barbara County, California.
83 pp./1984/paper 3561-2 $5.95

Passing the Health Care Buck: Who Pays the Hidden Cost?

JACK A. MEYER
with William R. Johnson
and Sean Sullivan

This study examines the phenomenon of the "cost shift" whereby the hospital costs that are not reimbursed by Medicare and Medicaid are shifted to privately insured patients. It analyzes the merits of alternative ways to finance the short fall in Medicare and Medicaid payments. The authors offer an incentives-based, market-oriented approach in both public programs and private insurance, an approach they con-

sider preferable to the regulatory model that has characterized most government policies in recent years.
49 pp./1983/paper 3528-0 $3.95

Market Reforms in Health Care: Current Issues, New Directions, Strategic Decisions

JACK A. MEYER, editor

The inexorable rise in health care costs has led to new
proposals for market reforms using incentives to change the
behavior of both consumers and providers. Sixteen chapters
examine all aspects of these proposals.

"This volume makes an excellent case for incentives and
describes their potential benefit. . . . Federal and state as well
as private solutions are defined and evaluated."
Journal of Policy Analysis and Management (second review)
331 pp./1983/paper 2236-7 $10.95/cloth 2242-1 $19.95

Economics and Medical Research

BURTON A. WEISBROD

With great advances in medical technology have come stag-
gering increases in medical costs. The solution to this cost
problem—health insurance—has itself contributed to growing national health expenditures. As an economist, Weisbrod
examines the causes and consequences of medical research
and suggests its appropriate role in the larger social system.

"The author brings to bear the wisdom gained from a long
and remarkably fruitful study of the economics of health care on
some painful choices confronting policy makers today. . . .
both instructive and sobering." *Southern Economic Journal*
171 pp./1983/paper 3512-4 $7.95/cloth 3513-2 $15.95

Controlling Medicaid Costs: Federalism, Competition, and Choice

THOMAS W. GRANNEMANN and MARK V. PAULY

High and growing Medicaid costs have led to demands to
control, limit, or cap program expenditures. This book iden-
tifies the sources of recent growth in Medicaid costs and
evaluates proposals for change.
112 pp./1983/paper 3515-9 $4.95/cloth 3527-2 $13.95

• *Mail orders for publications to:*AMERICAN ENTERPRISE IN-
STITUTE, 1150 Seventeenth Street, N.W., Washington,
D.C. 20036 • *For postage and handling, add 10 percent of
total; minimum charge $2, maximum $10 (no charge on prepaid orders)* • *For information on orders, or to expedite service, call toll free 800-424-2873 (in Washington, D.C., 202-
862-5869)* • *Prices subject to change without notice* •
Payable in U.S. currency or through U.S. banks only.